SHEFFIELD UNITED
Thirty Memorable Games
from the Seventies

First published in Great Britain in 2011 by The Derby Books Publishing Company Limited, 3 The Parker Centre, Derby, DE21 4SZ.

A catalogue record for this book is available from the British Library.

ISBN 978-1-85983-861-7

Printed and bound by Melita Press, Malta

NICK UDALL

SHEFFIELD UNITED
Thirty Memorable Games
from the Seventies

Acknowledgements

The author would like to express his thanks to Andy Pack and Sheffield United for permission to use the photographs, illustrations and excerpts from the club programmes. In particular I would like to thank my wife Doreen, for her patience and understanding during the research and writing of the book, and the great players of the 1970s, without whom there would be no fund of wonderful games and memories to make my work worthwhile.

Contents

The Campaigns of the 70s

1969–70

After their relegation from the First Division at the end of the 1967–68 season, United moved John Harris 'upstairs' to become general manager and brought in Arthur Rowley as the new team boss. Rowley had been brought in from Shrewsbury Town, but he had made his name in the game as a player, becoming the Football League's record goalscorer with 434 goals in 619 League games. Rowley brought in a raft of new signings who were to prove valuable acquisitions for the club: Ted Hemsley from Shrewsbury Town for £27,500; David Powell from Wrexham for £28,000; Eddie Colquhoun for £27,500 from West Brom, whom Rowley made captain, and, finally, record signing John Tudor from First Division Coventry City for £58,500. Just before he left, Rowley also brought in John Flynn from Workington Town for £5000.

The 1968–69 season saw the team suffer just three defeats at home, but they were only able to manage two away wins and finished in a disappointing final position of ninth. Crucially, Rowley had also sold fans' favourite Willie Carlin, the influential and diminutive midfielder, to Second Division rivals Derby County for £56,700 at the start of the season. Carlin helped Derby finish as champions of the division and, ultimately, gain promotion.

United prepared for the 1969–70 campaign with a pre-season tour of Holland. While the team were there, chairman Dick Wragg and John Harris flew out to resolve a dispute that the club was having with the players concerning incentives and bonuses. Unable to reach an agreement, Wragg and Harris do not seem to have been impressed when Rowley continued with his plans to take his players to a pony trotting race meeting at Hilversum. Rowley was known to be passionate about horse racing and there are suggestions that this did not make him popular with some sections of the Bramall Lane board. The fact was, however, that shortly after the team's return on 6 August, Rowley was sacked and Harris resumed the team manager's job.

The 1969–70 season was, nevertheless, embarked on with some optimism. The fans had faith in John Harris – who had won promotion with the Blades in 1960–61 – and United had a good squad. The team started the campaign in excellent form and raced to the top of the table. In the opening 14 League games United won nine, drew two and lost three. Four successive defeats in October, however, indicated that United were not the finished article. It became apparent as the season wore on that while the team were a strong proposition at home, and their points and goalscoring record at Bramall Lane were the best in the division, they still had not sorted out their away form. This was reflected in their campaigns in both Cup competitions. In the League Cup, United disposed of First Division Newcastle United 2–0 at the Lane, then Luton 3–0, but when they were drawn to play away at Leicester, they went down 2–0. The FA Cup saw a stirring 2–1 victory against eventual First Division champions Everton, but then the team suffered a dismal 3–0 defeat to Derby at the Baseball Ground in the fourth round.

At the top of the table at the end of January, the Blades were widely regarded as the best footballing side in the Second Division. The team was unable to fulfil their obvious potential, however, and four straight defeats in March effectively undid their promotion bid. United ultimately finished in sixth place four points behind Blackpool, who were promoted in second place. The season, therefore, proved a huge disappointment to Blades fans. Success would be expected next time around.

1970–71

Off the pitch, the 1970–71 season saw large strides made in United's attempts to raise revenue streams away from the football side of the business. Harold Rumsey, United's commercial manager, was responsible for the introduction of 'Lane Bingo' – the sale of 'Bingo' tickets with weekly prizes – and, most significantly, the development of the Lane Social Club. Before his appointment at Bramall Lane, Rumsey had been chairman and managing director of a Midlands brewery and had been involved in the setting up of the first social club in the English Football League. By the time the Blades' social club was established, eight others were also in existence for other teams. When phase one of the project – the Lounge Bar – opened at the start of November, it had captured the imagination of Blades supporters and was already over-subscribed. Importantly, United were moving with the times and challenging the old stereotypical picture of football as purely a man's game. Consciously, United's programme against Queen's Park Rangers on 14 November proudly declared that the new Lane Social Club was 'a place of comfort in which ladies can feel equally welcome'. Described as 'a first-class club in luxurious surroundings and with tasteful decor', phases two and three were also soon up and running and members were able to take advantage of the new 'Bier Keller' and 'Tudor Lounge Bar'.

Back row (left to right): Ian MacKenzie, Len Badger, Billy Dearden, Tony Currie, Geoff Salmons, John Tudor. Middle row: John Flynn, David Powell, P.G. Crawford, Alan Hodgkinson, Frank Barlow, Colin Addison. Front row: Pat Buckley, Alan Woodward, Eddie Colquhoun, Gil Reece, John Barnwell.

The need for extra revenue was not just to help to strengthen the playing squad; the desire to get a fourth stand at Bramall Lane was gathering pace. The 1967 AGM had voted to get rid of cricket at Bramall Lane to provide the Blades with a modern football stadium and, importantly, more seats in order to raise matchday revenues. The costs of building such a stand would be high, and every additional stream of income that could be generated would be extremely welcome.

On the pitch, United started slowly and without conviction, with poor performances and defeats in their first two away games against Orient and Norwich City. An impressive 1–1 draw at Cardiff on 2 September heralded the start of a 16-game unbeaten run that put the Blades firmly among the promotion front runners. Defeat at promotion rivals Luton in early December led to a period of inconsistent form that looked to seriously undermine United's promotion prospects. The danger that the Blades might fall away in the new year, as they had in the previous season, was needlessly feared, however, as John Harris moved decisively to reinvigorate and strengthen the team. On 27 January Harris and Dick Wragg negotiated a triple transfer in a series of meetings. Birmingham's tough-tackling midfielder Trevor Hockey was signed in order to add bite and leadership to the Blades team, along with goalkeeper John Hope and forward David Ford from Newcastle in exchange for striker John Tudor. The latter deal had proved more difficult as Harris had not initially wanted to part with Tudor, yet Magpies manager Joe Harvey was insistent. Ford had been an impressive player at neighbours Sheffield Wednesday but had lost form following a car accident; Harris hoped that he could recover it at Bramall Lane, although ultimately he never did. The key part of the exchange, however, was John Hope, who was brought in as a promising young 'keeper to take over from United legend Alan Hodgkinson, who had also suffered a loss of form. Hodgkinson's last League appearance for the Blades came at Bolton on 16 January and effectively marked the end of an era.

Hockey and Hope made their debuts at Oxford on 30 January, where United won 2–1, while Ford's debut was a week later in a 2–1 revenge victory over Luton Town at Bramall Lane. Yet it was to prove a tense period until the end of the season as the Blades lost key games to two of their promotion rivals: 1–0 at Carlisle on 27 February and 2–1 at home to Hull City on 9 March, the latter before a crowd of 40,227. The defeat to the Tigers would prove to be United's last, as they went unbeaten to the end of the season and finally secured second place – and promotion – in their final two games of the season. In an electric atmosphere at Bramall Lane, United despatched their main promotion rivals Cardiff City by five goals to one on 27 April, before sealing their promotion in euphoric scenes against Watford on 1 May with a 3–0 victory.

The Blades were now back where their supporters believed that they belonged, in the top flight. Having ended the season as Division Two's top scorers for the second successive season, United had shown their flair and attacking prowess – a reflection of their manager's positive footballing philosophy. The question was, would that be enough at a new, higher level?

1971–72

United went into the new campaign with a talented, but relatively small squad of players, and the size of the team would, ultimately, undermine the early promise of the season. Injuries or loss of form would inevitably mean that often replacements were not available or were not of the same high quality as the team's key men. Financially, without the ground development that could provide higher numbers of seats and increased revenue, United could not afford to reward their players with the level of wages that the most competitive top-flight teams could afford. Ted Hemsley, for example, was paid £60 a week, while comparable players elsewhere could be paid up to three times that figure. Len Badger's best wage during his career was £80 a week and Alan Woodward's was £110.

The playing squad was little changed over the summer. The only significant addition was Stewart Scullion from Watford for £25,000. The winger had turned down a chance to join the Blades two years earlier. Unfortunately, David Powell's recovery from injury had suffered a setback and he would not resurrect his Blades career.

After fears about the team's chances following a pre-season defeat against Twente in Holland, the side got off to a magnificent start. Undefeated in their first 10 League games, with eight wins and two draws, the Blades sat proudly at the top of the First Division. Having beaten the last three League champions – Leeds, Arsenal and Everton – Sheffield United were widely acclaimed as the best side to be promoted for many years. The winning run came to an end in a first- versus second-placed clash against Manchester United at Old

Trafford on 2 October. This was the first of a four-game losing run that saw the Blades lose the top spot. At the turn of the year, however, they were in fourth place and still had every chance of obtaining a place in Europe. Ambition on the field was also increasingly reflected off it. Commercial manager Harold Rumsey announced his intention to get 1,000 Development Fund agents, and a 'Fourth Side Sub-Committee' of the board of directors was holding regular meetings to discuss the financial implications of building a new seating stand on the Bramall Lane cricket pitch. Reflecting on United's overall situation, the *Green 'Un's* Peter Howard declared, 'I think it is fair to say that in 1971 Sheffield United supporters have not had it so good for a long, long time.'

Yet the New Year proved to be disappointing as United were knocked out of the FA Cup 3–1 at home by Second Division Cardiff City on 15 January, and two weeks later they were heavily defeated 5–0 by Arsenal at the Lane. After those defeats the Blades were not really in a position to challenge for a European place as the team suffered from some inconsistent performances. There were still some exciting games, however, and some good football was played, including an exciting 3–3 draw with Manchester City and a Billy Dearden hat-trick against West Ham in February, while 45,000 came to the Lane in early April to see the 1–1 draw with Manchester United. The 4–0 home defeat to eventual champions Derby on 8 April seemed to underline the fact that the Blades just did not have the depth of squad, unlike their competitors, to maintain their European ambitions. Yet a final position of 10th had established the Blades as a competitive and solid top-flight outfit. One positive was that the season saw the debuts of Mick Speight, Steve Goulding, Ian MacKenzie, Alan Ogden, Steve Cammack, Ian Holmes and Tom McAlister, and some of these youngsters were to prove valuable additions to the side in the future.

1972–73

The Blades, with a season's experience in the First Division behind them, were looking to improve on their mid-table position as the new campaign began. The squad, although still small in terms of the number of seasoned campaigners, looked in fairly reasonable shape. Keith Eddy had been signed for £50,00 from Watford, Trevor Hockey had recovered from the broken leg that he had sustained against Manchester City, John Flynn was close to a return from injury and first-team experience had been given to several promising young players.

Before the campaign began in earnest, United reached the Final of the pre-season Watney Cup, only to lose on penalties to Bristol Rovers. They opened their League campaign with an impressive 2–1 away victory at promoted Birmingham City, yet the optimism created by this result, achieved without the suspended Tony Currie, did not last for long, as key injuries to Eddy, Salmons and Scullion exposed the frailties of United's small squad.

After beating Arsenal 1–0 at the Lane on 7 October United won just once in their next 12 League games, a return that left them facing the threat of relegation. A mini-revival in

Back row (left to right): Coxon, Staniforth, Faulker, Cammack, Holmes, Goulding, Ogden. Third row: Hodgkinson, Coldwell, Barlow, Powell, Flynn, Salmons, McAlister, Hope, MacKenzie, Badger, Hemsley, Speight, Short, Goodall. Second row: Currie, Woodward, Dearden, Colquhoun, Harris, Scullion, Hockey, Ford, Reece. Front row: Ward, Allan, Williams, Conroy, Ludlam, France, Brooks.

form in January seemed to have lifted the pressure, but a poor February brought the gloom back to Bramall Lane. A significant problem for John Harris was finding another striker to score goals and give support to the excellent Billy Dearden. The manager hoped that he had found the answer when he signed Alan Warboys from Cardiff City, in exchange for David Powell and Gil Reece. Warboys proved ineffective, however, and the goalscoring problem was only resolved when Jim Bone was signed from Norwich City in February, in exchange for Trevor Hockey and £30,000. Scotsman Bone proved an inspired signing by Harris as he struck up an immediate understanding with Dearden and the two went on a scoring spree that effectively drove the Blades to safety from relegation. Important, too, was the emergence of Keith Eddy. Finally throwing off his injury problems, Eddy returned to the side in January and, once match-fit, proved to be an excellent addition in midfield. In fact, it was Eddy's form that prompted Trevor Hockey to look for a move, and so Eddy assisted the Jim Bone transfer.

At the end of April United were in the media spotlight as they dared to win 2–1 at Old Trafford on the occasion of Bobby Charlton's final home game before his retirement. The season ended with the Blades in 14th place, unable to improve on the previous season's League performance, but two players did enjoy key seasons. Young Tom McAlister, at 19 years of age, assumed the goalkeeping duties and had a superb season. The Scot looked as if he would go on to tie down the position for years to come, a true successor to Alan Hodgkinson. Billy Dearden, as dangerous to opposition defences as ever, hit 20 League goals and is, to date, the last Blade to score that many goals in the top flight.

Yorkshire v Lancashire, 7 August 1973.

1973–74

The close season brought little in the way of additions to the United playing squad. Colin Franks was signed from Watford for £55,555, but he was to play a very limited role in his first season. United lost their opening two games, at home to promoted Burnley and away at Wolves, but played well, and John Harris was insistent that the team would come good. The start of September, with a 2–1 victory at Chelsea and a 5–0 thrashing of Arsenal at Bramall Lane, again indicated that United could be brilliant and prove to be a handful for any First Division team. Yet, as in the previous season, results proved to be inconsistent and the Blades ultimately looked destined to be a mid-table team.

Certainly, fortune was not on United's side, as Keith Eddy broke his collar bone in late September and Tom McAlister broke his leg while playing against Manchester City at Bramall Lane on 20 October. The injury was to prove a personal tragedy to the young Scot, who, ultimately, would not regain the first-team jersey at Bramall Lane. The goalkeeping position was to prove problematic, both John Connaughton and the returning John Hope proving unequal to the task. Up front, too, the Blades were struggling, as the Dearden–Bone partnership that had terrorised defences at the end of the previous season proved ineffective.

Back row (left to right): Steve Goulding, Len Badger, Ted Hemsley, John Hope, John Connaughton, Tom McAlister, Tony Currie, Ian MacKenzie, Colin Franks. Front row: Alan Woodward, Geoff Salmon, Stewart Scullion, Eddie Colquhoun, Billy Dearden, Keith Eddy, Jim Bone, John Flynn.

The new South Stand under construction.

One positive was the emergence of Mick Speight in midfield. Given an opportunity by the injury to Eddy and the loss of form and subsequent transfer of Stewart Scullion, Speight proved a capable player and appeared increasingly in the first team.

The beginning of December heralded the end of an era at Bramall Lane with the appointment of Ken Furphy from Blackburn Rovers as United's new team manager, with John Harris again moving upstairs. Furphy, a younger 'track suit manager', was seen by the

Chairman Dick Wragg and John Hassall.

board as the man to take the side into a new era. Media-savvy Furphy made his home debut with a 4–2 win against Southampton on 22 December. Furphy publicly declared his ambition to make Sheffield United a 'Super Club', one of the best in England, but privately he realised that this would be very difficult, with United's commitment to building the new South Stand meaning that there would be little in the way of finances to strengthen what would soon become an ageing side.

The New Year brought United injury problems, which weakened the team and never allowed them to rise above mid-table. Talisman Tony Currie missed five games in February, as well as the last seven of the season, and John Flynn was also injured during February and March. Crucially, the Blades were without Billy Dearden for the whole of the latter part of the season, following his injury at White Hart Lane in early January. Billy had effectively seen his best days, and although he would return next season, he was never again to reach the heights of his earlier career at United.

Disappointingly, again the Blades failed to make significant progress in the FA Cup, going down 3–2 in the third round at Ipswich. Given the financial constraints on the club, this was not good news. Furphy did strengthen the squad, however, bringing in Terry Garbett for £30,000 and Tony Field for £76,666 from Blackburn Rovers, his old club. Most importantly, the manager signed Jim Brown for £70,000 from Chesterfield. Brown finally solved the goalkeeping problem, proving a reliable and competent performer who would go on to play for Scotland.

1974–75

In Ken Furphy's first full season managing the club, money was exceptionally tight due to the interest charges on loans raised for the building of the new South Stand. This had a key impact on the financing of the playing squad. During the close season, United had sold Geoff Salmons to Stoke City for £180,000. As Salmons was regarded as a crucial member of the team, the fans felt that he had clearly been sold to help balance the books. The mood of the supporters was not helped by the fact that United only made one new signing, and that was David Bradford, a utility player from Blackburn who cost just £10,000. As a significant number of United's first team were around the age of 30, there were concerns that several players were close to being past their best. The lack of quality player reinforcements, made many supporters fear that the club would face relegation at the end of the season.

At the beginning of the season Dick Wragg stepped down as club chairman to further pursue his role as chairman of the FAs International Committee. Wragg was officially replaced by John Hassall on 20 August, and on the following day the new chairman travelled with the players to the game at Newcastle. Moving with the times, the new team coach was 'equipped with the modern conveniences of television and stereo in order to help the players overcome the tedium of longer away journeys'.

Back row (left to right): S. Goulding, E. Hemsley, S. Faulkner, S.H. Conroy, J. Brown, T. McAlister, L. Badger, T. Garbett, C. Franks, A. Ogden. Front row: A. Woodward, D. Bradford, T. Field, K. Eddy, A. Currie, E. Colquhoun, W. Dearden, T. Nicholl, M. Speight, G. France.

Given their concerns over finance, attendances became a crucial issue for the board. With their heavy investment in the new South Stand, real team strengthening could only occur if attendances approached an average of 30,000. This proved problematic all season, especially as there was a feeling among many supporters that the team was not good enough and, as a consequence, gates were suffering. As a result, there was little chance of additions to the playing squad and, importantly, United also had to shelve plans for the building of an indoor training facility. Neither did it help that attendances were falling across the game. This reflected a national trend that would not be effectively reversed until the much-later introduction of the Premier League. An important impact on attendances, too, was the continuing and seemingly growing problem of hooliganism. This was particularly important as increasing numbers of parents, concerned about the safety of their children at football matches, stopped them from attending.

In trying to address this latter problem, manager Ken Furphy deserved great credit for his forward thinking. At the start of the season he issued an appeal to all Blades fans to respect the opposition and their fellow supporters, to act sensibly on away trips and to make Sheffield United welcome visitors at every ground in the country. What marked Furphy out, however, was his groundbreaking EDS club, initiated early in 1975. This was a club for young supporters who, as members, were given special coaches to away grounds, were chaperoned by responsible adults and met and protected by the local police at away grounds. The first such trip was to Carlisle on 8 February 1975 and was a great success. Furphy made clear to parents that membership of the EDS club was a guarantee that their children would be safe at games. Furphy was keen to develop a sense of belonging and responsibility to the club among young fans, and the EDS had gatherings at which he and some of the players were present. In effect, Furphy was trying to foster a sense of social responsibility at a time when many critics felt that the traditional social values were collapsing all around them. Within a few weeks there were over 150 young members of the EDS club, and at home games they gathered at the bottom of the Kop.

As for the football, many pundits believed that the Blades were one of the relegation favourites when the season kicked-off in August. Yet United made a solid start, losing only one of their first seven League games, which suggested that they could prove to be more than just a mid-table side. The 3–1 victory over Ipswich on 31 August was particularly pleasing, and Tony Fields' solo goal in that game lives long in the memory of those privileged to see it. A 5–1 defeat at Leeds in late September put matters back into perspective, however, and a poor run through part of November and early December had the critics again declaring that the Blades would end up in relegation trouble. Yet a splendid victory at Tottenham on 18 January launched United on a splendid run of form that lasted until the end of the season, and for a time Ken Furphy and many optimistic supporters believed that the Blades could actually end up as League champions. Ultimately it was not to be, as United fell four points short of title winners Derby and narrowly failed to secure a place in Europe. They did have a big say in the final destination of the title, however, and their home victory over Stoke and away victory at Everton effectively ended both of those teams' title aspirations.

It had been a magnificent season for United, and the players had probably over-achieved. One concern, however, was that expectations had risen enormously and the frailty of United's position was not fully appreciated. The reality was that the team's ageing squad was another year older, and with crowds only rising at the very end of the season, the club still lacked the finances to significantly strengthen the squad.

1975–76

The new season began with real optimism from all quarters at Bramall Lane: directors, management, players, supporters and the local media. The tremendous finish to the previous season, which had seen the Blades lose just two out of their last 19 fixtures, had brought the club within a whisker of European qualification, and there was real optimism that the team could push on again in the coming campaign.

The Blades, however, were a team in transition. The issue of players approaching, or passing, their peak, which had been noted at the start of the previous season, still had not been adequately addressed, although manager Ken Furphy was clearly aware of the need to restructure the side. Unfortunately for Furphy, the financial constraints created by the new South Stand – opened on the first day of the new season – and the disappointing attendances for the vast majority of last season were biting hard and severely limiting his room for manoeuvre in the transfer market. United simply could not afford to acquire the calibre of First Division players necessary to push the team on to the next level. Furphy

Back row (left to right): S. Goulding, E. Hemsley, T. Garbett, S. Conroy, T. McAlister, J. Brown, S. Faulkner, E. Colquhoun, C. Franks. Middle row: A. Hodgkinson (reserve team coach), K. Murphy (team manager), L. Badger, P. Nugent, R. Hill, J. Flynn, A. Woodward, S. Cammack, T. Field, C. Coldwell (first team coach), D. Turner (youth team coach). Front row: D. Bradford, M. Speight, C. Guthrie, K. Eddy, A. Currie, W. Dearden, S. Ludlam.

had, like John Harris before him, been forced to look in the lower divisions for reinforcements since arriving at the club back in December 1973. His key signing for the new campaign was again a lower-division player, unproven at top-flight level. Chris Guthrie cost almost £90,000, not an insignificant sum to the Blades but well behind the financial clout of many of their top-flight rivals. A tall and powerfully built centre-forward, Guthrie had scored 35 goals in 108 League appearances for the Shrimpers, and Furphy hoped that he would prove able to finish off the chances created by Currie and Woodward. Importantly, Billy Dearden's best days were now clearly behind him and United were desperate to find a spearhead for their attack. Yet ultimately the policy of buying in the lower divisions produced average signings, Guthrie himself failing to live up to the promise of his debut against Derby County on the opening day. Unfortunately Furphy did not seem to have John Harris's ability to find a succession of rough diamonds that could be coached and developed in order to shine at a higher level. This compounded the problem that United were still relying on players who had been at Bramall Lane for a significant period of time to continue to carry the hopes of the club. Ultimately, such players, through the effects of time, injury and loss of form, would be found wanting. Unfortunately, the 1975–76 season would be the point at which this occurred.

To be fair to Ken Furphy, he had begun to divert the club back towards an emphasis on youth development, a policy that had served so well in the 1960s but which the club had moved away from. The establishment of Moncrieff House, a Victorian property in Nether Edge, which acted as a club residence for new apprentice players, had been one initiative to try to attract new young talent, and Furphy was hopeful of bringing home-grown players through to the first team. Pleased with developments so far, Furphy told the share holders' AGM in August 1975 – just prior to the start of the new season – that United's young prospects were coming along well, and that in 18 months there should be fewer worries about the strength of the forward line. He was eventually proved right, with Keith Edwards, Simon Stainrod and Imre Varadi all emerging. But unfortunately for the manager this was a policy that required time, and time was not on his side.

The Blades started the season well, drawing 1–1 against champions Derby County at Bramall Lane in a competitive and entertaining match on 16 August. There was no sign of what was to follow as the Blades went into a disastrous run of results that saw them lose their next seven League games, before finally registering a 2–1 victory against Burnley at the Lane on 23 September. Hopes of a recovery were dashed, however, as they lost their next two fixtures and Ken Furphy was dismissed on 6 October. His replacement, Notts County manager Jimmy Sirrel, proved unable to retrieve the situation and there was a run of 19 League games before victory was achieved again on 14 February against Aston Villa. In an unhappy situation, United were clearly headed for relegation, with Sirrel unable to wave the magic wand that could save them. Significantly, it was also clear that the new manager was unable to establish good relations with the senior players and there were stories of fraught and difficult training sessions. Tony Currie, United's star player, was a constant source of

Admission prices during the 1975–76 season.

It's 'All Ticket' for Manchester United

For the visit of Manchester United to Bramall Lane on Saturday, 13th December, 1975, it has been decided to make this an all-ticket game.

In the interests of safety and crowd control, the Bramall Lane end standing area and West Terrace in John Street have been allocated completely to Manchester United fans. Blades supporters are asked to co-operate and help the club by using the John Street East Terrace area and Spion Kop.

Tickets for this match are available from our Ticket Office during normal office hours.

Spion Kop, Ground ...	...	65p	John St., Centre	£1.70
Special Juvenile Enclosure ...		40p	John St., Front Centre ...	£2.15
(pass holders only)			Bramall Lane	£1.50
Senior Citizens ...	...	40p	Juveniles (under 14 years)	75p
East Terrace, John Street	...	75p	New South Stand, Wing ...	£1.50
Stands:			Juveniles (under 14 years)	75p
John St. Wing Stand, Rear	£1.20		New South Stand, Centre	£2.15
Senior Citizens	...	60p	New South Stand, Special	
John St. Wing Stand, Front	£1.50		Centre Enclosure ...	£2.50
Juveniles (under 14 years)	75p		(100 seats only)	

Postal applications are invited but the correct remittance must be enclosed, together with a stamped addressed envelope.

Save 25% on season tickets purchased by 31st May

	Day Ticket Prices	Gross Season Ticket Value to nearest 50p	25% discount till 31.5.76	15% discount after 31.5.76
New South Stand, Centre, Adult	£2.15	£45.00	£33.75	£38.25
New South Stand, East & West Wings, Adult	£1.50	£31.00	£23.25	£26.35
New South Stand, East & West Wings, Juvenile	£0.75	£16.00	£12.00	£13.60
John Street, Stand Front Centre, Adult	£2.15	£45.00	£33.75	£38.25
John Street, Stand Centre, Adult	£1.70	£36.00	£27.00	£30.60
John Street, Stand Front East & West Wings, Adult	£1.50	£31.00	£23.25	£26.35
John Street, Front East & West Wings, Juvenile	£0.75	£16.00	£12.00	£13.60
John Street, Stand East & West Wings, Adult	£1.20	£25.00	£18.75	£21.25
Bramall Lane Stand, Adult	£1.50	£31.00	£23.25	£26.35
Bramall Lane Stand, Juvenile	£0.75	£16.00	£12.00	£13.60
Terrace, Adult	£0.75	£16.00	£12.00	£13.60
Ground, Adult	£0.65	£14.00	£10.50	£11.90
Terrace, Juvenile	*	£10.50	£7.87	£8.92
Ground, Juvenile	£0.40	£8.50	£6.37	£7.22

Special Season Ticket Concessions only for Senior Citizens

New South Stand, East & West Wings	*	£16.00	£12.00	£13.60
John Street, Front East & West Wing	*	£16.00	£12.00	£13.60
Bramall Lane Stand	*	£16.00	£12.00	£13.60
John Street, East & West Wings	£0.60	£12.50	£9.37	£10.62
Terrace	*	£10.50	£7.87	£8.92
Ground	£0.40	£8.50	£6.37	£7.22

* Indicates no Day Tickets available at concession rate for these areas.

To obtain the maximum discount (25%) this application must be in the hands of the Club Secretary with full remittance by Monday, 31st May, 1976; also to ensure the same seat(s) are allocated as held previously. (If for any reason you are unable to apply early—a telephone call giving your requirements will help.)

Existing Season Ticket holders have now received their 1976-77 renewal application form by post.

All applications should include payment and full instructions regarding tickets required. To qualify for a juvenile privilege applicants must be under 14 on 21st August, 1976. Documentary evidence for senior citizen concession must be produced.

Remember — applications to be with the Secretary by Monday, 31st May, 1976.

The Secretary, Sheffield United F.C., Bramall Lane, Sheffield, S2 4SU.

Telephone 25585 or 730630

Name ....

Address ....

....

Enclose Cheque/P.O. value .... No. of Tickets .... Stand Section ....

Application form for a 1976–77 season ticket.

transfer speculation and had put in a transfer request following Furphy's departure from the club. The board continued to refuse Currie's request to leave, but clearly, as relegation became certain, it was inevitable that he would depart for pastures new. Although 'TC' played out the season at the Lane, other senior players did not. Len Badger, Ted Hemsley, Keith Eddy and Tony Field all departed along with younger, but experienced players, such as

Tom McAlister and Steve Cammack. In addition, coach Alan Hodgkinson departed to join Gillingham. Sirrel's decision to let such experience go, rather than try to rebuild the team spirit and purpose that had served the club so well in the previous season under Furphy, was questionable at best. With no depth to his squad, Sirrel increasingly threw in younger players such as John McGeady, Steve Ludlam, Keith Edwards, Simon Stainrod and Tony Kenworthy, but it was too soon and at too high a level, and the season could not be saved.

At White Hart Lane on 27 March, with six games still to go, United were relegated, a confirmation of the inevitable. Sirrel accepted responsibility for the relegation, declaring, 'I'm the manager of the club and we have been relegated. Therefore I have a deep sense of personal failure.' Clearly it was not all the manager's fault, given that he had inherited such an extremely difficult position, so he was perhaps being too hard on himself. Worrying, however, was his bold statement that 'If I had to do it all again, I don't think I would have changed anything I did.'

With the Blades enjoying a relatively successful end to the season – four wins and a draw in their last six games – there was some optimism for the coming campaign. Promising young players had performed well in these games; Alan Woodward, although not Tony Currie, were still at the club; and Jimmy Sirrel had an excellent record of building a side with promotion potential in the Second Division, as he had done on a shoestring budget for Notts County at Meadow Lane.

The final game of the season, at home to Birmingham on 4 May, was a stark reminder of United's fall from grace. A year earlier Blades fans had travelled in their thousands to St Andrew's for the final fixture of the season, which almost saw United qualify for Europe. The goalless draw that day was not enough to secure European success, but Blades fans were riding on a wave of optimism. A year later that optimism had been cruelly smashed. With Birmingham needing a result to guarantee that they would avoiding joining United in the Second Division, and with the fixture being the Blades' farewell to the top flight, an excellent crowd of 30,782 was in attendance to see a 1–1 draw. On that day in May 1976, few Blades fans in attendance could imagine that Alan Woodward's strike would be United's last goal in the top flight for another 14 seasons.

1976–77

United started the season with a very different squad from that of 12 months ago. The huge but inevitable loss was Tony Currie, who had departed to Leeds for £245,000. There was no Keith Eddy, Tony Field or Terry Garbett. They had all departed for the North American Soccer League, where they again joined up with manager Ken Furphy at New York Cosmos and, impressively, Pele. Badger and Cammack were with Chesterfield, McAlister was with Rotherham and Billy Dearden had returned to Chester. Ted Hemsley, effectively frozen out under Sirrel, would depart for Doncaster at the season's end.

Back row (left to right): Garner, Franks, Colquhoun, Brown, Conroy, Stainrod, Flynn, Calvert. Front row: Whittle (released), Ludlam, Hamilton, Guthrie, Woodward, Kenworthy, McGeady, Bradford, Johnstone.

With no real money available – Currie's sale helping to balance the books – United's recruitment of players, predictably, had to be carried out on a low budget. The problem was compounded by the inevitable drop in crowds brought by playing football in the Second Division. Sirrel did sign the experienced Aston Villa forward Ian 'Chico' Hamilton for £40,000, John Cutbush from Fulham for £10,000 in March 1977, Dennis Longhorn from Sunderland for £22,500 in October 1976 and Steve McKee for £25,000 from Linfield in December. Yet none of these players were outstanding, and the ability to unearth gems from the lower divisions at bargain prices, as John Harris had done, was one that current boss Jimmy Sirrel – like Ken Furphy before him – did not seem to possess while at the Lane. On the other hand, the season did see the emergence of the promising young players identified by Ken Furphy before his departure. Keith Edwards, Tony Kenworthy, Simon Stainrod, John McGeady and Gary Hamson – who became, for a time, United's youngest League debutant when he played at Cardiff aged 17 years and 67 days on 30 October – all made significant contributions to the season. The Blades were not about to win anything, however, if they relied too much on their young players. This was clearly illustrated by their two-goal defeat to Luton on the opening day of the season at Kenilworth Road. The United line up included 20-year-old Paul Garner, 21-year-old Steve Ludlam, 18-year-old John McGeady and 17-year-old Simon Stainrod.

The Blades did not achieve a victory until their fifth League game, and they managed just two wins in their first 11 matches. Yet they still had club captain Alan Woodward and, as he entered his 30th year, his skill and experience were a great asset to the team. One of the highlights of the campaign was when 'Woody' surpassed Derek Pace's post-war scoring record with his 141st League goal at the Lane against Bristol Rovers on 18 December. A great achievement for one of United's most experienced players was mirrored by one of its youngest; on 12 April Keith Edwards goal against Blackpool at Bramall Lane was his 11th in eight consecutive games – another club record. Young Edwards was on his way to becoming the Blades legend that his older colleague, Alan Woodward, already was.

Yet, ultimately, it was a disappointing season. United had never looked like mounting a serious promotion charge, whereas Wolves, relegated with them the previous season, ended the season as champions and on their way back to the top flight. Furthermore, manager Jimmy Sirrel's position looked under threat at times, particularly in the period following the victory over Chelsea on 3 December. That result raised expectations that United might mount a serious charge for promotion, yet the team went on to win just two of their next 12 League games, and in early March they looked in danger of being pulled into a relegation struggle. But chairman John Hassall retained faith in Sirrel's ability to get it right at the Lane and gave the manager his backing. Seven wins and two draws in their last 14 games had seen the club safe, but clearly the manager's position had been weakened by the experience and his team would need to do far better next term.

Yet there remained one positive. The youngsters had gained a season of experience, and as there was still no money to spend, the club would be looking to that younger generation for improvement in results in the future.

1977–78

The new season began with Sirrel unable to significantly strengthen the squad. Steve Ludlam was moved on to Carlisle United for £16,200 and Chris Guthrie to Swindon Town for £22,000. In came Bobby Campbell, a young striker from Huddersfield Town, for

Back row (left to right): Cec Coldwell (trainer), Cliff Calvert, John Flynn, Dennis Longhorn, Chris Guthrie, Steve Conroy, Jim Brown, Eddie Colquhoun, Colin Franks, Tony Kenworthy, Jimmy Sirrel (manager). Front row: Gary Hamson, John Cutbush, Mick Speight, Alan Woodward (captain), Ian Hamilton, Simon Stainrod, Steve McKee, Paul Garner, Keith Edwards.

£10,000. The budget buy was indicative of the financial problems United were in, and much faith would again be put in the development of the club's young players.

The season, however, started disastrously. Following an acceptable defeat at newly-relegated promotion favourites Tottenham on the opening day and victory over Hull at the Lane in the following fixture the Blades went on a dismal run. After losing four and drawing one of their next five League games – well beaten 3–0 at home in the League Cup by Everton and then 3–0 by Sirrel's old team, Notts County, in the Anglo-Scottish Cup – the manager's time was up. This time, chairman John Hassall did not support him, and Jimmy Sirrel was dismissed on 27 September. To give the board the time to find the right successor, chief coach Cec Coldwell was put in temporary charge of the team as caretaker manager.

Sirrel's reign had been one of continual decline, and as the *Green 'Un's* Tony Pritchett noted after the manager's departure, 'His failure at Bramall Lane is as amazing as his success at Notts County had been remarkable.' Yet perhaps Notts County, a club that had much lower expectations than Sheffield United, and where he took over a club in the League's basement rather than in the top flight, allowed him the opportunity to put his personal imprint and way of doing things on the players, which was not possible at a club of established 'stars'. Sirrel's approach to training and coaching, with Cec Coldwell having relatively little input in terms of ideas, was seen as rather basic in some quarters. Mostly, training consisted of practice matches – usually the first against the second XI – and there was criticism that such repetitive sessions were uninspiring and that the development of players' technique was neglected. Perhaps, in his early days at the club, Sirrel found dealing with First Division footballers a more complex task than he was used to and failed to understand the need to respond to individuals differently. Just after his appointment, Sirrel had told Tony Pritchett that it had taken him just three weeks to institute his methods and get the players to respond after joining Fourth Division Notts County, and that he hoped to do the same at Bramall Lane. That comment does suggest his lack of sophistication. With less ability, the County players were not independently minded, were more in need of direction and were far less inclined to question their manager's ideas than the squad that Sirrel inherited at Bramall Lane.

It was Coldwell's second time as caretaker manager. Prior to Sirrel's arrival he had presided over two games – defeats to Wolves in Division One and Hull City in the League Cup. It was anticipated that United would find it hard to find the right manager, so Coldwell was likely to be given a longer temporary role this time. With a great start to the post-Sirrel era, the board was fortunate in being able to have significant space before settling on a successor. Coldwell, switching to a smart suit from his trademark tracksuit on match days at the insistence of the players, lifted morale in the dressing room and tightened up the defence, and the players certainly responded to him. Senior players Jim

Brown, John Flynn, Eddie Colquhoun, Chico Hamilton and John Cutbush all played at a higher level and with greater enthusiasm, and this helped to pull United out of the crisis. Promotion contenders Southampton were defeated 3–2 on 1 October in Coldwell's first game in charge, and the Blades went on an unbeaten run of eight games, including five wins. They continued in good form, losing just three of their next nine games, with a 6–1 victory at Cardiff on 3 December and the fightback at Bramall Lane from two goals down to draw with Spurs on 2 January being two of the highlights.

While there was some talk among the fans and the media that Cec, with 26 years at the club as a player and coach under his belt, may be given the job on a full-time basis, it seems that Hassall and the board were, increasingly, focusing upon Harry Haslam at Luton. Haslam was a manager who had dealt with serious financial constraints, was a real wheeler-dealer in the transfer market, showed a clear profit on his transactions and had shown an ability to unearth real talent, such as Malcolm Macdonald and the Futcher twins. After the Blades suffered three successive five-goal defeats in January – to Arsenal in the FA Cup and Bolton and Sunderland in the League – Haslam was appointed manager on 26 January.

Coldwell had brought the best out of his older pros like Flynn, Colquhoun, Brown, Hamilton and Woodward, and had encouraged the development of increasingly influential young players such as Kenworthy, Edwards, Hamson and Stainrod. As such, the team had recovered well and, at the turn of the year, was seriously thought to be on the fringes of the promotion race. The heavy defeats against Bolton and Sunderland put matters into perspective, however, and it is unfortunate that Coldwell's temporary reign ended on this note. Yet Bolton and Sunderland were top teams and Coldwell had certainly put the Blades in a position where early-season fears of relegation were long gone. This allowed the board the luxury of taking time over their new appointment, and it also gave Haslam breathing space to assess the playing squad and to introduce new South American methods in training and the style of play. It meant that the season could be seen out with a mid-table finish, as United won six and drew three of their last 16 games under their new boss.

In appointing Haslam, the club's board had made one of its most crucial decisions for the future of the club. After the inability to find a stable management team since the departure of John Harris, everyone associated with Sheffield United was praying that this time the board had got their appointment right.

1978–79

United grabbed all the national headlines prior to the start of the season thanks to Harry Haslam's capture of Alex Sabella from the River Plate Club in Buenos Aires, Argentina. Argentina had hosted the 1978 World Cup Finals during the close season and Haslam, aided by his Argentinian coach Oscar Arce and the mediation of Antonio Rattin –

Back row (left to right): G. Goodall (physio), C. Coldwell (chief coach), C. Calvert, A. Keeley, T. Smith, C. Renwick, C. Franks, J. Brown, S. Conroy, S. Stainrod, S. Finnieston, B. McGarry, I. Varadi, R. Bate (coach), O. Arce (coach), N. Briggs (chief scout). Middle row: K. Edwards, M. Guy, J. Cutbush, P. Garner, G. Hamson, D. Bergara (assistant manager), H. Haslam (manager), A. Woodward, M. Speight, S. McKee, A. Sabella, A. Kenworthy. Front row: K. Larner, P. Champken, K. Matthews, R. Harwood, J. Flood, T. Dickey, G. Clark, I. Benjamin, P. Jones.

Argentina's infamous captain from the 1966 World Cup Finals – had travelled to Argentina to secure affordable, top-quality players. Close to signing Osvaldo Ardiles or Ricky Villa, who had played in Argentina's World Cup-winning team, Haslam settled on Sabella's signature after losing out on the former two players to Tottenham. The connections made by Haslam in Argentina created hopes that future South American talent could be brought to Bramall Lane. Importantly, the signing of Alex Sabella provided a huge lift to the morale of Blades supporters and, consequently, many were enthusiastic about the club's prospects as the campaign got under way.

Similarly, prior to the start to the season both Harry Haslam and his board of directors were bullish about United's prospects. In reviewing the events that had followed the appointment of Haslam in January, United's programme for the opening fixture against Orient on 19 August declared that Haslam had 'created a new atmosphere by adopting a more virile approach to training and raising the standard of play with the infusion of new talent, not only at Football League level, but by catching youngsters.' The manager, continued the programme, had a proven track record 'of having accomplished much with meagre resources', and his recent activities in South America exhibited an 'imaginative approach' and 'showed that Sheffield United was in the forefront so far as farsightedness was concerned'. Importantly, Haslam had given the club back its pride: 'People are now sitting up and taking notice. They realise that Sheffield United are doing things in a big way.' This would mean that the Blades would be moving up the League table and making a real impact in the Second Division after the disappointments of the previous two seasons.

Haslam's own optimism came through in an interview in the *Green 'Un* on 18 August. Haslam declared that when he came to the club in January it was initially a matter of introducing new training techniques under South American assistant manager and director of coaching Danny Bergara, and getting the players to play good football by 'using the ball'. The close season then gave Harry the opportunity to use his skills in negotiation, and Haslam was adamant that in bringing Argentinian Alex Sabella to the club, along with Steve Finnieston from Chelsea and Peter Anderson from Tampa Bay – the latter formerly with Haslam at Luton – he had the personnel who would provide United with a good footballing side that would perform powerfully in the Second Division. But what they also needed was consistency, and if that were to come then the team would have every chance.

Haslam was at pains to point out that Sabella was 'not here to carry the club' and that there would be a real team effort. Having spent significantly – buying Finnieston for £90,000, Alex Sabella for £160,000 and, shortly after the start of the season, John Matthews for £90,000 and Nicky Johns for £150,000 – Haslam's wheeling and dealing was required to re-balance the books. As a result, out went John Flynn to Rotherham for £15,000, Bobby Campbell was given a free transfer and, most importantly, Keith Edwards was sold to Hull City for £55,000 prior to the start of the season. Edwards' transfer was a major surprise to Blades fans, given that the young striker had only just turned 21, had been the top scorer with 18 goals two seasons ago and had scored 11 times in the previous campaign. It seemed that Haslam was sacrificing real potential for questionable experience, and when Finnieston proved injury-prone and managed just 23 appearances and four goals during the season, Haslam's decision truly seemed to have backfired. The later sales of other young prospects – Imre Varadi for £85,000 to Everton and Simon Stainrod to Oldham for £60,000 – again brought into question the logic of Haslam's dealings.

The season itself certainly did not get off to the flying start that the fans had expected, with a 2–1 home defeat to Orient on the opening day. But then the team enjoyed two promising away performances – a 1–0 win at Leicester and a 2–2 draw at Preston – followed by a morale-boosting 1–0 victory over Liverpool in the League Cup. Significantly, Alan Woodward moved to Tulsa Renegades in America at the beginning of September and he was a great loss to the side. The growing inconsistency of the team was illustrated by the fact that, after the Liverpool game, they proceeded to lose three of their next four games before going undefeated in the subsequent four. United played very well at second-placed Stoke City on 28 October, losing a very close game 2–1, yet surprisingly that game was followed by a period of serious decline in which the Blades lost five out of six League games. Successive home victories against Cardiff and Newcastle either side of Christmas gave promise of a recovery, but it proved a false dawn as United went 10 games without a win in the period up to the end of March. Indicative of United's poor form was their desperate 3–1 defeat at Aldershot in an FA Cup third-round replay.

Hopes of recovery from the threat of relegation coincided with the loan signing of Bruce Rioch from Derby County at the end of March. The Blades defeated Bristol Rovers 1–0 and

West Ham 3–0 at home in Rioch's first two games, and the team won four games and drew one during his eight-game loan spell with the club. After Rioch left, United won 2–1 in a crucial game against relegation rivals Charlton at the Lane on 28 April. That game should have secured United's position, and with three games to go, two of them at home against Blackburn and Leicester, the club's destiny was in their own hands. Yet the Blades lost to a 10-man Blackburn side that had already been relegated, and then defeat at Cambridge United and a final 2–2 draw against Leicester – a pitch invasion by frustrated young fans failing to stop the inevitable – meant that, for the first time in their history, United would be playing in the third tier of English football. Astounding for the football world, at that time, was the fact that both Sheffield clubs would now be playing in the Third Division.

1979–80

United began their first-ever campaign in the Third Division with Haslam again having been active in the transfer market during the close season, hoping this time that his signings would bring more success. Len de Goey, a Dutch midfielder, was brought in from Sparta Rotterdam for the significant sum of £125,000, defender Tony Moore was signed from Burton Albion, strikers Barry Butlin from Peterborough for £15,000, Argentinian Pedro Verde from Alicante and Jeff Bourne from Atlanta Chiefs for £35,000. The need for forward talent was abundantly clear given that Peter Anderson had left the club following relegation and Steve Finnieston had undergone an operation and was expected to be unavailable for some time, although in fact Finnieston never played for United again. True to his reputation for wheeling and dealing, Haslam sold Gary Hamson to Leeds United for £140,000 and, after appearing in the first three games of the new season, teenager Ian Benjamin was sold to West Bromwich Albion for £125,000. The money for Benjamin, who had only played a handful of games, was impressive, but was yet another indication that the policy implemented under Ken Furphy and Jimmy Sirrel to develop young talent – one that was so strongly backed by chairman John Hassall at the time – had been abandoned. It was clear that the initiative to build for the future was now being replaced by the policy of securing more experienced professionals. Whether these players had the ability or commitment to help United succeed, however, remained to be seen.

Gary Hamson's departure to the top flight, given his proven quality over more than 100 League games for the Blades, was perhaps inevitable, but the sales of Edwards, Varadi, Stainrod and Benjamin over the previous 12 months were not. Haslam was, however, showing a healthy profit on his transfer dealings, a profit that would have been even greater had Alex Sabella departed for Second Division Sunderland for a reported offer of £600,000. Sabella, however, decided that he only wanted to move to a top-flight club, and he ended up staying at the Lane for the whole season.

United were installed as promotion favourites by the bookmakers, and the national newspapers were very optimistic about the Blades' chances of success. On paper, their defensive qualities were good. There seemed strength in depth, with MacPhail, Kenworthy, Matthews, Tibbott, Garner, Cutbush and Speight, plus Moore, Renwick, Jones and Casey as cover. Midfield and attack looked rather more problematic, however. Much would depend on midfield and on Dutchman Len de Goey making a quick transformation to the very tough physical demands of the third tier of English football. Up front, Bourne and Butlin were experienced enough to perform well at this level, but neither looked as if they would become prolific scorers. Significantly, United had only one first-choice goalkeeper in Stephen Conroy, and Haslam would later have to juggle with three other goalkeepers – Neil Ramsbottom, Terry Poole and Derek Richardson – in an attempt to replace him.

Pre-season went well for United as they gained three 1–0 victories in the group stages of the Anglo-Scottish Cup against Mansfield Town, Cambridge United and Notts County. The season itself saw a win, a draw and two defeats in the first four games, and then a great run of nine wins in their next 10 games, which seemed to mark United out as champions elect as they swept to the top of the table with a healthy 24 goals scored. Yet at the end of October the team's fortunes began to change, as results became inconsistent and were probably a more realistic reflection of the team's potential. In their next eight League games, leading up to Christmas, they won three, drew one and lost four. That early great run, however, kept them at the top of the table, giving Blades fans a continued, but perhaps false, sense of optimism.

The loss of Steve Conroy, following a broken arm at the start of December in the Anglo-Scottish Cup defeat at St Mirren, did not bode well for the stability of the defence. Replacement 'keepers Neil Ramsbottom and Derek Richardson, the latter signed from Queen's Park Rangers for £50,000, looked anything but confident. The crunch came with a visit to Hillsborough to play neighbours Sheffield Wednesday on Boxing Day. A Third Division record crowd of 49,309 attended, but United's cause was not helped by an early injury to Mick Speight. A goal down at half-time, the Blades ended up losing 4–0. A draw and a victory against promotion contenders Grimsby Town and Blackburn Rovers at Bramall Lane followed the Boxing Day debacle. These two results suggested that United could maintain their position at the top of the table. The reality was different, however, and in three games United had played the sides who were eventually promoted. Ironically, Jack Charlton, who turned around Sheffield Wednesday's fortunes, had been available when the Blades were searching for Jimmy Sirrel's successor, and he was being touted in some quarters as an ideal appointment to the Bramall Lane hot seat.

Following the New Year's Day victory over Blackburn, United won just three and lost 10 of their last 20 League games. Finishing in 12th position, their form in the latter part of the season, if not for their excellent start, would have seen them relegated. Next time, the Blades would not be so lucky.

Sheffield United 2–1 Everton
FA Cup third round

3 January 1970

The 1969–70 season was the second season back in Division Two after relegation from Division One in 1968. With John Harris replacing Arthur Rowley as manager just days before the season began, there was potential for upheaval, yet Harris's long association with the club meant that supporters had good grounds for optimism. John Harris had led the Blades to promotion in 1960–61 and they had a good squad. The team flew out of the blocks, with six wins, a draw and just one defeat in their first eight games. October, however, indicated frailties with four successive defeats, yet the promotion show was back on track by the time of Everton's visit in the FA Cup in early January. In this period United had achieved some impressive League victories at Bramall Lane: 4–0 against Blackburn, 5–0 against Aston Villa and 6–0 against Birmingham. In fact, United were exceptionally strong at home. Prior to Everton's visit they had won 10, drawn two and lost just once in the League at Bramall Lane and had defeated First Division Newcastle in the League Cup. Yet away from home, they were weak. A record of three wins, four draws and seven defeats threatened to undermine their promotion prospects.

United went into the game at second place in the Division Two table, behind the eventual champions Huddersfield Town. Everton were second in Division One and would ultimately go on to win the title by nine points. Blades fans were thus savouring the prospect of a fight against one of the country's top sides, and they believed that their team had a chance of winning. The match, therefore, attracted an attendance of 29,116 to Bramall Lane, over 12,000 up on the season's average gate. The attendance was an indication of the Blades fans' desire to get back to playing matches against the footballing elite. As the match programme noted, 'Bandying about these club names proves the class in which we play today, a class which we are eager to rejoin. Everton are one of the really great teams and better than when we met them last.'

The Everton side were managed by Harry Catterick, well known to Sheffielders as he had managed Wednesday before leaving them for Everton in spring 1961. Under Catterick, the Toffees had won the League Championship in 1962–63 and the FA Cup in 1966, ironically against Wednesday. Everton had also been FA Cup runners-up in 1968 when they lost to West Bromwich Albion. John Harris had noted on hearing the Cup draw that 'it couldn't have been more attractive or difficult for us.' A glance at the Everton team underlined his point; noted as one of the wealthiest clubs in English football during that era, the team contained several high-profile acquisitions, including 'keeper Gordon West, who commanded a record fee when signed from Blackpool in March 1962; Howard Kendall, signed from Preston in March 1967; and World Cup-winner Alan Ball, who cost £110,000 from Blackpool in August 1966. In addition, Keith Newton – England's left back – had just been signed from Blackburn Rovers in mid-December.

There did not seem to be a single chink in the Everton armour. They had an excellent defence and a dynamic and brilliant midfield containing Colin Harvey, Alan Ball and future Blades boss Howard Kendall. The player making all the news, however, was young striker Joe Royle. At 20 years of age, Royle headed the list of First Division marksman with 15 goals, and many were predicting that he had a huge future as an England international. Although Everton were a powerful team, however, they had suffered recent defeats at the hands of Liverpool and Leeds and had slipped to second in the table. With United's strong home form, there was hope at Bramall Lane that the Blades could get a result.

The United squad was unchanged for the third successive game. They had hoped that Welsh international David Powell may return to the side following injury, but he still had not returned to training, so John Flynn continued in the side. Pleasing for Blades fans was the fact that Tony Currie had overcome a leg injury, suffered in the game against Watford, and was available to play. 'Keeper Alan Hodgkinson had reached the significant landmark of playing in his 50th FA Cup match for the club, having missed just one since he played his first in 1957. The Everton squad was unchanged from their game against Leeds.

The team line ups were as follows:

Sheffield United: Hodgkinson, Badger, Hemsley, Barlow, Colquhoun, Flynn, Woodward, Currie, Addison, Salmons, Reece. Substitute: Tudor (not used)

Everton: West, Wright, Newton, Kendall, Labone, Jackson, Whittle, Ball, Royle, Hurst, Morrissey. Substitute: Brown

Referee: Mr J.K. Taylor

Attendance: 29,116

As the teams turned out to the strains of *Ilkley Moor*, United's entrance music at that point in time, they were met by pleasant winter sunshine and a Bramall Lane pitch that had been liberally sanded.

The game kicked-off with Everton defending the Shoreham Street End, with United preferring to attack the Kop in the first half. It was the visitors who had the first meaningful chance when a misplaced pass from Alan Woodward was seized upon by Tommy Jackson. The Everton man played a superb through ball, which Hodgkinson, smartly off his line, was able to snatch away from the onrushing Alan Whittle. Soon, however, it was the Blades who were on top, determined to give full rein to their attacking capabilities. Colin Addison fired in a shot from the tightest of angles, the ball deflected off Everton's John Hurst and over 'keeper Gordon West's despairing dive and against the bar, with Gil Reece putting the rebound wide. The Toffees' luck seemed to be holding as Alan Woodward dispossessed Henry Newton and, racing away, hit a thunderous shot against the angle of bar and post with West well beaten. With the Lane crowd completely fired up and roaring their heroes on, Wright's last-ditch header cleared Woodward's dangerous in-swinging corner.

After a quarter of an hour Everton were clearly shell shocked; United's power, aggression and fine attacking play was completely overwhelming their illustrious opponents. Yet, cruelly and against the run of play, it was the visitors who took the lead. After 17 minutes Len Badger failed to control an awkward cross from Whittle and John Morris sped into the area to pick up the ball and, as he rounded Hodgkinson, was brought down for a penalty that was coolly converted by Alan Ball. The goal lifted Everton, who now began to have a greater share of the play. Hodgkinson was forced to save a testing low shot from Tommy Wright, and a sweeping move downfield ended with Ball passing to Joe Royle, who shot wide. Yet the Blades had their moments too, especially when Woodward, fed by Barlow, shot through a crowd of players, the unsighted West showing lightning-quick reactions to scramble the ball around the post for a corner. After 33 minutes a

Gil Reece heads United level against Everton.

Colin Addison scoring the second goal against Everton.

shocking incident saw an accidental collision of heads in the Everton penalty area between Gil Reece and Tommy Wright. Play continued for a while, until the latter collapsed with blood all over his face. Wright, stretchered off and needing stitches in a deep wound over his right eye, was immediately replaced by substitute Sandy Brown, who took up the left-back position with Newton moving over to the right. Reece, able to walk off the pitch, returned after a few minutes having had two stitches inserted into the top of his head. As half-time approached, United again established their dominance and were close to achieving parity as Currie headed Badger's free-kick against the bar.

As United re-emerged for the second half, the game reached a crucial point. Having hit the woodwork three times and been on top for much of the game, the Blades could have been forgiven for losing their resolve. Yet, as David Jones noted in the *Sheffield Telegraph*, the team pressed on, 'Constantly switching the points where they applied pressure, [Sheffield] never gave Everton a moment's rest and, more essentially, never relied on one source of inspiration, which would have given the methodical Everton team a chance to devise a counter plan.'

After five minutes Bramall Lane erupted as the Blades scored their equaliser. Barlow played a short pass out to Woodward on the right, whose long centre was met 12 yards out by Gil Reece, whose header flew past West and into the corner of the net. United's left-winger now clearly had the bit between his teeth. A last-ditch tackle denied him a chance on goal as he continued to weave through the Everton defence until Howard Kendall brought him down inside the area. Players and fans screamed for a penalty, only for their appeals to be waved away by referee Jack Taylor. It was Tony Currie who then took over, riding three tackles and feeding Geoff Salmons, only for the latter to shoot wide. A Hurst volley that dipped just over the bar was a reminder of the visitors'potential, and the match was, noticeably, entering a phase in which Everton were beginning to pose more of a physical challenge. Yet Eddie Colquhoun was marshalling his defence superbly, shackling the dangerous Royle in expert fashion. Flynn, Badger and Hemsley were tackling with purpose and belief, and in consequence it was United's attacking threat that was providing a far more potent challenge to the Everton defence. Curry continued to be a real menace, and it was he who, after 79 minutes, started the decisive move that saw United take the lead and, ultimately, the spoils. A great ball out to Woodward on the right saw the winger outpace Labone and head for the dead-ball line, from where he cut back a superb cross that, evading the Everton defence, was met by Colin Addison, who flew through the air to head the ball into the back of the net.

It was a brilliant victory for United, and their performance was applauded on all sides. It was one of the most pulsating games seen at the Lane for many years, a brilliant fightback and two splendid goals against the country's top team. *The Star*'s reporter, Peter Howard, declared, 'I have tried hard over the weekend to recall a more exciting Blades display in nearly 10 years of covering the club's affairs, but I cannot.' Manager John Harris agreed, 'I think this was the finest performance by a United team in my 10 years with the club. It was wonderful.'

They performed impressively, but the Blades were to be disappointing in the fourth round, going out 3–0 to Derby County at the Baseball ground and showing little of the fighting qualities evident at the Lane. In fact, hopes for promotion were to flounder thanks to the club's poor away form. Topping the table prior to their game at Derby, United, regarded by many as the best footballing team in Division Two, could find no consistency away from the Lane, achieving just six wins and three draws in their 21 away fixtures, and ultimately finishing the season in a disappointing sixth place, four points behind second-placed – and promoted – Blackpool.

Match 2

Sheffield United 3–3 Bristol City
Division Two

5 September 1970

The start of the 1970–71 season saw much optimism among the supporters that United would go up. It was a view shared by many of the pundits, both local and national, who thought that United looked likely champions of the division. These assessments were based on the fact that the Blades had kept their best players, and their staff had been strengthened by the arrival of John Barnwell and Billy Dearden. With the Blades having played some superb football in the previous campaign, it seemed that if they could improve on their away form, promotion would be assured. Notably, off the pitch, the new season saw United open their new Lane souvenir shop on John Street. A range of official club souvenirs could now be purchased by the fans; money raised through club operations away from the football pitch was becoming increasingly important as a way of enhancing the club's finances.

Bristol City at home was the fifth game of the League campaign, and things had not got off to a good start. United had been defeated 3–1 by Orient on the opening day, 15 August, but had then beaten Swindon 2–1 at home the following week, suggesting that the team was fine. Defeated 1–0 at Norwich on 29 August, however, United put in a truly awful display, and although a creditable 1–1 draw was achieved at Cardiff in midweek, prior to the Bristol City game the Blades were back in 18th position and had only three points. In an atmosphere of growing concern, manager John Harris, attending the shareholders' annual meeting prior to the trip to Cardiff, remarked that he was not happy with all the

Listed below are just a few souvenirs which are on sale at the Lane Shop in John Street.		**SEASON TICKETS**
United Car Stickers	1/6	
Key rings	1/-	*There are a few*
Ashtrays	6/-	*Season Tickets*
United Ball Pens	1/-	*still available*
Teddy Bears	38/6	*and may be*
Duffle Bags	15/-	*purchased from*
Holdalls	21/-	*the Cherry Street*
Rosettes	3/-	*Office.*
Programmes	1/-	
Team Mate Slippers	26/-	
United T Shirts	from 9/-	
Soccer 'Jamas	from 36/-	
Football Boots	from 31/-	

We are happy to announce the new "Lane Souvenir Shop" which is open in John Street. The shop will be open on all match days, with a full range of official club souvenirs on sale and is well worth a visit. This range will be added to in the following weeks. Binders will be on sale shortly in the Lane shop for your collection of Lane Line Up and Central Line Up.

Listed below are just a few souvenirs which are on sale at the Lane Shop in John Street.		**SEASON TICKETS**
United Car Stickers	1/6	
Key rings	1/-	*There are a few*
Ashtrays	6/-	*Season Tickets*
United Ball Pens	1/-	*still available*
Teddy Bears	38/6	*and may be*
Duffle Bags	15/-	*purchased from*
Holdalls	21/-	*the Cherry Street*
Rosettes	3/-	*Office.*
Programmes	1/-	
Blades' Autograph Books	2/6	
Team Mate Slippers	26/-	
United T Shirts	from 9/-	
Soccer 'Jamas	from 36/-	
Football Boots	from 31/-	

The shop is open on all match days, with a full range of official club souvenirs on sale and is well worth a visit.

Binders will be on sale already in the Lane shop for your collection of Lane Line Up and Central Line Up.

KAREN CUTS THE TAPE ...

Sheffield pop singer Karen Young cuts the tape to open the new Sheffield United souvenir shop in John Street. Next to her is Christine Hague, who is Miss Cancer Research, and also pictured are Sheffield United players. On right of the picture is Barry Glynn—whose firm were responsible for the shop alterations, standing next to him is Harry Marsh Lane Shop manager.

Sheffield pop singer Karen Young and Christine Hague, Miss Cancer Research, provide the glamour as the new souvenir shop is opened on John Street.

talk of promotion, even though it was clearly the club's objective. He declared that expectation and pressure were clearly unsettling many of his players. Nevertheless, they would just have to learn to deal with it.

Peter Howard, writing in the match programme against Bristol City, reflected similar views to the manager, 'Many people believed United were better placed for a promotion push than was the case at the start of last season. Football is full of pressures, both on and off the field, yet successful clubs have to live with them.'

United's draw at Cardiff, another team fancied for promotion, had been hard-fought and suggested that the Blades were potentially back on track. The team had played well, but Tony Currie had taken a knock on his knee and John Barnwell had been absent with an ankle injury picked up in the previous game at Norwich, and both were rated as doubtful to face the Robins. So too was Ted Hemsley, who had strained a thigh muscle at Cardiff. Fortunately, all three were declared fit to play.

The United camp was suffering some upset, however, from a pair of transfer requests put in a fortnight earlier by winger Gil Reece and striker Colin Addison. Reece's request had been immediately turned down, yet Addison's had not been considered by the board until its meeting on Thursday night. Turning down Addison, the board informed the media that 'The request was rejected because, at the present time, we simply cannot afford to let Addison go.' It was suggested that Addison's request had followed a disagreement with coach Cec Coldwell, and chairman Dick Wragg indicated that manager John Harris was 'smoothing things over' between the two. The decision to keep Addison, who had not played since the opening day at Orient, which was probably the true reason for his request, was seen as essential due to worries that injuries could easily weaken the playing squad. The only change to the line up from the Cardiff game saw Geoff Salmons coming in for Frank Barlow in midfield. Barlow was a more defensive player than Salmons and not as well suited for the more attacking formation that Harris preferred to use at home.

Bristol City were entering the game with the reprimands of their manager, Alan Dicks, ringing in their ears. On four points from four games, City had lost at Leicester and Dicks had criticised their 'indiscipline', saying that 'the way we gave goals away was dreadful.' Pleasing for the Robins manager was the fact that talented young inside-forward Chris Garland would return to the side following his absence with an ankle injury at Leicester. Defenders Dickie Rooks and Trevor Jacobs did not overcome the injuries that they had picked up at Filbert Street, however, and were replaced by Stacey and Connor.

Sheffield United: Hodgkinson, Badger, Hemsley, Powell, Colquhoun, Salmons, Woodward, Barnwell, Currie, Reece. Substitute: Tudor (replacing Barnwell)
Bristol City: Gibson, Stacey, Drysdale, Wimshurst, Connor, Parr, Skirton, Garland, Galley, Gow, Sharpe
Referee: Mr B.J. Homewood
Attendance: 15,097

United started the game on the front foot, going on to overwhelm the City defence with a succession of attacks. Playing well on top, it seemed only a case of when, rather than if, United would convert one of their many chances. Yet after 25 minutes the breakthrough had failed to come and disquiet was beginning to emerge on the terraces. Two minutes later the unthinkable happened, as United's 'keeper, Alan Hodgkinson, uncharacteristically dropped the ball at the feet of centre-forward John Galley, who gratefully struck the ball into the net to put the visitors a goal up. Galley's physical presence was clearly causing some discomfort to the United 'keeper, but his fellow defenders were also having something of a nightmare game as two further goals were gifted to the visitors after half-time, with Galley scoring five minutes after the break and Gerry Gow after 64 minutes. At this point there seemed to be no way back for the Blades as they struggled to find any semblance of order or pattern to their play. Bill Thornton of the *Sheffield Telegraph* reflected the disbelief of the fans present, who questioned 'how this team of such proven prowess, conquerors of champions Everton last season, could allow themselves to play so badly for a near 40 minutes of pure misery.'

With some of the Lane crowd beginning to jeer their team, preparing to reassess their optimism for the season ahead, Alan Woodward launched an unlikely revival. After 67

Billy Dearden, after scoring United's second goal against Bristol City, heads back to the halfway line to get on with things.

minutes the right-winger raced to the edge of the penalty area and unleashed a ferocious shot into the roof of the net, thereby raising the hopes of his fellow players and of the Blades fans. Tony Currie, who had been impressive throughout, now took charge, urging the team forward with a series of surging runs into the heart of the Robins defence, probing and searching for opportunities to shoot himself, or to play in one of his fellow

Alan Woodward jumps for joy after John Tudor saves a point with his equalising goal in injury time.

forwards. The substitution of the out-of-sorts John Barnwell by John Tudor also brought new vigour to the forward line. It was Tudor who linked with Tony Currie to lay on the second Sheffield goal for Billy Dearden after 72 minutes; it was the centre-forward's first goal for the club. Yet, as the remaining minutes ticked away and United's attack failed to find the equaliser, it seemed that their brave comeback would be thwarted. But, with just two minutes to go, Woodward again raided down the right and put a great cross into the box. As the ball eluded those in the area, left-back Ted Hemsley, who was up in support of the attack, acrobatically sent the ball back across the goal with an overhead kick and John Tudor, who was first to react, hooked the ball into the net. The goal rescued a point for the Blades and both crowd and players danced around in disbelief and excitement.

It had been a pulsating game, 'a storybook revival which had to be seen to be believed', according to *The Star*'s Peter Howard. There were still question marks hanging over the United team, however. Could they find the necessary consistency in their performances to put themselves firmly into the promotion race? Thankfully, the game provided the impetus that the team needed. The fightback raised morale, and just three days later United took on Leeds United in the second round of the League Cup at Bramall Lane, with the First Division leaders going down to a single Tony Currie goal in front of a near 30,000 crowd. The team's new-found confidence was taken into the League programme, the fightback against Bristol City providing a pivotal point in the season's promotion campaign, as the Blades went unbeaten in their next four games and began to climb the League table prior to city rivals Sheffield Wednesday's visit to Bramall Lane on 3 October.

Sheffield United 3–2 Sheffield Wednesday Division Two

3 October 1970

Following their victory over Leeds, opposition manager Don Revie, impressed by the Blades' display, declared that United would 'walk the Second Division'. Revie's confidence seemed well-placed as United began to put together a string of solid performances, winning two and drawing two of their next four matches. This included a thumping 5–1 victory over Portsmouth at Fratton Park on 30 September, the Wednesday evening prior to the Bramall Lane derby. Instrumental in the run was the form and growing maturity of Tony Currie. Scorer of a brilliant winner against Leeds, the midfielder, still only 20 years old, was named a reserve for the England Under-23 match against West Germany on 14 October at Leicester. Currie had played, and also scored, in the England Under-23 matches against Wales and Bulgaria during the previous season.

United's good run had seen them move up to sixth place in the League table, with 10 points from nine games. This put them three points behind top club Leicester. Wednesday were 11th with nine points from 10 games. Off the field, work at Bramall Lane was well underway on the new luxury Lane Social Club. Applications for membership were now available: 7 shillings and sixpence for an individual; 10 shillings for a husband and wife; and five shillings for pensioners and season ticket holders. Everything off the field was gearing up to raise more revenue for the club's promotion push.

United's new luxury social club

is nearing completion. Application forms
for membership are available in the Pools Office and
Cherry Street Pavilion.
Membership 7/6
Husband and Wife 10/-
O.A.P. Season Ticket Holders 5/-

Lane Social Club – Bier Keller.

The Players' Lounge.

Fans of both Sheffield clubs were eagerly awaiting the first derby match for three years. All the seats were sold well in advance of the match and the local media were steadily building up the tension towards Saturday's showdown. United were the favourites and were particularly buoyant following their victory at Fratton Park, where Alan Woodward had proved to be the star man by hitting a hat-trick against Pompey. Manager John Harris was relishing the prospect of the derby, declaring that 'our lads have got the bit between their teeth just now and they are very determined.' In terms of player availability, Harris's hand was strengthened by the fact that Eddie Colquhoun and Alan Hodgkinson were both available following their absence at Fratton Park. Graeme Crawford had replaced 'Hodgy', while striker John Tudor had been brought in as a makeshift, yet impressive, centre-half, to replace Colquhoun. For his starting XI, Harris restored Hodgkinson and Colquhoun to the line up, with Tudor moving to the substitutes' bench.

Wednesday, following the previous season's relegation from the First Division, were failing to make a real impact on the Second Division. They had won just three of their first 11 games and were in a disappointing mid-table position. Owls manager Danny Williams had been appointed in summer 1969 and had presided over the team's fall from the First Division. He had seemed an inspired choice by the Wednesday board, having led Third Division Swindon to promotion and a famous League Cup Final victory over Arsenal at Wembley. Yet Wednesday's poor start to the season meant that he was now feeling the pressure. In his pre-match press conference, Williams reacted in an irritable fashion to the questions put to him. Asked about the make-up of the Wednesday side he replied, 'Nobody knows yet. The man who is in is the first to be told. And I'll tell him, not the papers.' When asked about United's great win in midweek and the likely impact it would have on their performance in the derby game, Williams tetchily declared, 'So United got five in midweek, what's that got to do with tomorrow's game? In football it's the next game that counts, not the last one.' Williams was hoping to increase competition among his players by selecting his 12-man squad early for the game, with only 'keeper Peter Grummitt told that he would definitely start the game. Interestingly, the Wednesday team would contain Alan Warboys, later signed by the Blades, and Sam Ellis, later assistant manager to Kevin Blackwell at Bramall Lane.

Although it seemed that most commentators felt that the Blades were strong favourites to win the game, the local bookmakers did not necessarily agree. The Blades were even money to win, Wednesday 2:1, while 5:2 was on offer for the draw. The odds had not been changed in light of the Blades' midweek victory, and the odds were a clear signal that, as usual, the form book tended to go out of the window where the passionate frenzy of a local derby was concerned.

Sheffield United: Hodgkinson, Badger, Hemsley, Powell, Colquhoun, Barlow, Woodward, Reece, Dearden, Currie, Salmons. Substitute: Tudor (replacing Reece)
Sheffield Wednesday: Grummitt, Thompson, Young, Todd, Ellis, Craig, Sinclair, Prendergast, Downes, Warboys, Sissons.
Referee: Mr P. Partridge
Attendance: 38,983

In front of their biggest home crowd for three years, the Blades played towards the Kop in the first half. An interesting statistic was that they had not yet scored at that end that season. The early stages of the game were dominated by the Blades. Wednesday started with just three at the back – Thompson, Ellis and Young – a key mistake, as they were soon being torn to pieces by United forwards Woodward, Dearden and Reece. After just six minutes the Blades were in front. Ellis fouled Dearden, Woodward floated the free-kick to the far post, where the unmarked Eddie Colquhoun headed the ball down and past Peter Grummit. Five minutes later the Blades were two up, as Alan Woodward crossed from the right and Billy Dearden stole in between Sam Ellis and Alan Thompson to head home.

It looked to be all over for Wednesday. With Woodward and Dearden in rampant form and threatening a rout, however, manager Danny Williams responded by dropping Sam Todd to right-back and switching Steven Downes to midfield and Tommy Craig to centre-forward. The changes were inspired, as they denied United's front men the space that had brought their early success and tightened up the Owls presence in midfield, where Prendergast and Downes began to stifle the creative talents of Currie. Slowly but surely, the visitors began to impose themselves on the game. A warning of the emerging danger posed

Substitute John Tudor fires home the winner against Wednesday.

by the battling visitors came after 44 minutes, when Jack Sinclair missed an excellent chance after being set up by some fine interplay between Thompson and Prendergast. Continuing to play well after the break, the first period of the second half saw the Wednesday revival reach its peak. After 57 minutes Eddie Colquhoun knocked the ball into his own net for an own-goal as he tried to clear from Craig. Six minutes later came a superb equaliser as Prendergast slipped a pass inside Ted Hemsley and Jack Sinclair ran onto it to shoot past Hodgkinson from an acute angle.

Wednesday's stunning recovery was to be their downfall, however, as it finally shook the Blades out of their lethargy. The catalyst for the Blades' victory was substitute John Tudor, brought on to replace Gil Reece, who brought a new urgency up front. Almost immediately the striker combined with Currie to create a great chance for Salmons, and then after 74 minutes Dearden broke away from Thompson's tackle. As a scramble

United's Alan Woodward weaves through the Owls defence with Bill Deardon looking on.

ensued in the Wednesday area, John Tudor smashed the ball through Grummitt's legs and into the net. Wednesday were rocked by Tudor's goal, but by no means broken, and they still came back at their opponents. A frantic assault on United's area saw Hodgkinson and Warboys out cold on the ground as Powell headed Craig's resultant effort over the bar. Not finished, the Blades stormed back, Tudor almost making it four when he acrobatically hooked the ball back from a narrow angle and hit the post. It was the final meaningful act of a highly entertaining and competitive derby. The Blades had the spoils, defeating their fierce rivals by three goals to two.

Defeat was hard on the Owls after their excellent fight back, Williams declaring, 'when it was 2–2, I reckoned we were going to win.' Proud of the spirit of his players, he continued, 'Don't tell me [United] eased off and let us off the hook. They were concerned in the second half about our comeback. We didn't let them come at us.' Harris was clearly relieved and was pleased to win. Nevertheless, he was concerned at how his players had seemingly 'switched off' and allowed Wednesday back into the game. 'We had Wednesday on the floor, but allowed them to get up', remarked United's boss.

Harris was now set on ensuring that the Blades kept focused and consistent throughout the 90 minutes. United had certainly turned the corner. Although, following their heroics against Leeds, they were to be knocked out of the League Cup at White Hart Lane by First Division Tottenham Hotspur on the following Wednesday night. They were not defeated in the League, however, until they lost 2–1 to promotion rivals Luton on 5 December. This meant an unbeaten run of 16 games, which put United up to fourth place, a point behind the second promotion place.

Unfortunately for Williams, although he told the Wednesday board on his arrival at the club that it would take four years to turn the club around, he was unable to raise the Owls above a mid-table position and, having gone out of the FA Cup at Tottenham, in early January he was sacked.

Sheffield United 5–1 Cardiff City Division Two

27 April 1971

With two games left to play in the 1970–71 Second Division campaign, the table stood as follows:

	Played	Points
Leicester City	40	55
Sheffield United	40	52
Cardiff City	39	51

Back then, with two points for a win and one for a draw, and with United playing Cardiff, Leicester needed just one more point to be certain of promotion. For the Blades, given that Cardiff had a game in hand, they just had to win the fixture. Cardiff would, of course, be content with a draw, as this would keep the promotion issue in their own hands.

The Blades had gone eight games undefeated since the fractious game against Hull City at Bramall Lane on 9 March, where they were defeated 2–1 in front of 40,227 supporters. It had been a hard-fought succession of games, including tough draws gained at Queen's Park Rangers, Leicester, Sheffield Wednesday and Middlesbrough, and with home victories against Blackburn, Millwall and Birmingham City. Crucially, United had shown that they had the character, allied to their undoubted talent, to finish the job. The whole team had toughened up, perhaps a result of the strength introduced into midfield following John Harris's signing

Trevor Hockey being interviewed by Yorkshire TV's Richard Whiteley shortly after signing for United.

of Trevor Hockey from Birmingham in late January. The defence had been magnificent, going seven games without conceding a goal until Middlesbrough's John Hickton had scored in the previous Saturday's 1–1 draw with the Blades at Ayresome Park.

Earlier in the season, United and Cardiff had shared the points in a 1–1 draw at Ninian Park on 2 September. The game followed a dismal defeat for the Blades at Carrow Road, after which the critics were circling around the United camp. It was a display that had galvanised the team, sending them on a run of 16 unbeaten matches.

Cardiff had done remarkably well. They had sold star striker John Toshack to Liverpool in November for £110,000 – a record for both clubs. Toshack, just 21 years of age, had already scored over 100 goals for the Bluebirds, and so his departure was expected to undermine their promotion campaign. But Toshack had been replaced by Alan Warboys from Sheffield Wednesday at the end of December, and the City team had continued to perform well. With regular forays into Europe – winning the Welsh Cup brought them participation in the European Cup-Winners' Cup – the Bluebirds had won admirers abroad. Real Madrid manager Miguel Munoz, whose team had played Cardiff, declared that they were a side of true First Division quality. Cardiff were certainly strong away from home. They had won eight and drawn six of their 19 away matches. Leicester manager Frank O' Farrell noted that 'their great experience in the European Cup-Winners' Cup has made them into a strong away side.' With a reputation as a team that could put 10 men behind the ball and as a team that could grind out results, many pundits felt that Cardiff would arrive at Bramall Lane intent on securing the point that would hand them back the initiative with their game in hand.

The tension was certainly building in Sheffield. As Peter Howard noted in *The Star* that day, 'It is a measure of the tightness of the division that after 40 matches the Blades should be in a position where nothing is sure, where everything is still required of them.' No one wanted a repeat of the disappointment against Hull City, and the rallying call went out from club and local media to the fans to do whatever they could to roar their favourites on to the needed victory. United boss John Harris declared in *The Star*:

> We know we have a rare fight on our hands tonight. We have worked hard for nine months – now it will all depend on 90 minutes. But we are more than ready.

Nothing would give me greater pleasure than promotion for the sake of the club, the fans and the city. There is no doubt in my mind that our supporters have helped put us where we are. I regard the supporters as part of our team. We need a real United effort tonight and if we get some frustration early on, as is possible, I hope the fans will show patience and give us all the backing they can. Their support could help us break through.

With the Blades expecting another bumper 40,000 crowd, fans were being urged to arrive early and use all the turnstiles around the ground to avoid overloading them prior to kick-off. Seats were also made available in the cricket pavilion – a distant view, but a guarantee of getting in. Meanwhile, a special train had been arranged from Cardiff, an unusual departure for an evening fixture, to bring in the visiting support, an illustration of the fact that excitement was just as great in South Wales for the fixture.

The United squad was unchanged from the draw at Middlesbrough, although the attacking abilities of David Ford were swapped for the more defensive ones of Frank Barlow. Cardiff had a scare over the fitness of Alan Warboys, but fortunately for the Bluebirds, he was declared fit to play. Key midfielder Brian Harris, who had been injured over Easter, although included in City manager Jimmy Scoular's 15-man squad, proved unable to make the matchday 12.

Sheffield United: Hope, Badger, Hemsley, Flynn, Colquhoun, Hockey, Woodward, Salmons, Dearden, Currie, Reece. Substitute: Ford
Cardiff City: Eadie, Carver, Bell, Sutton, Murray, Derrett, Gibson, Clarke, Phillips, Warboys, King. Substitute: Woodruff
Referee: Mr F.M. Nicholson
Attendance: 42,963

From the moment that the teams emerged onto the field, the atmosphere was incredible. With nearly 43,000 packed into the Lane, the Blades were roared on from the start. Contrary to all expectations, the match ended up producing some spectacular attacking football, clearly helped by the fact that the Blades got off to a flying start, hitting a couple of quick goals and so ending any plans Cardiff may have had of keeping the game tight by playing defensively for a point.

It took the Blades just six minutes to open the scoring, when Trevor Hockey played an oblique pass behind the Bluebirds' defence for Billy Dearden to turn home for 1–0. Continuing to take the game to Cardiff, and spurred on by the confidence gained from their early strike, the Blades continued to threaten and the visitors were hard pressed to hold them at bay. After 33 minutes the Blades had a second goal, as a Tony Currie free-kick

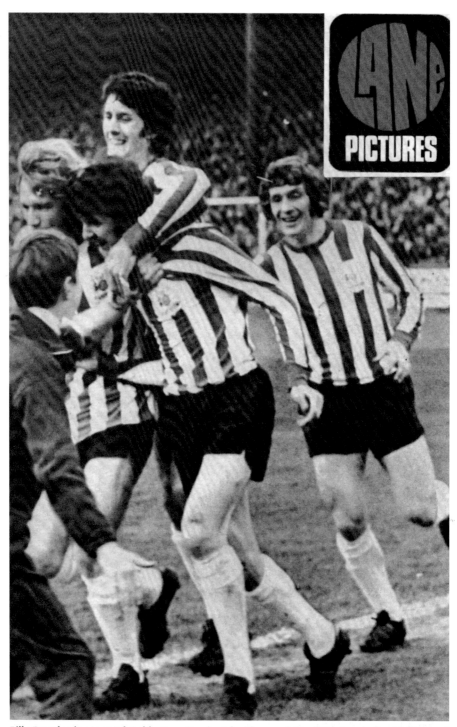

Billy Dearden is congratulated by Tony Currie, John Flynn and Alan Woodward after his first goal against Cardiff City.

was helped into the area by Len Badger for John Flynn to head home. It seemed that City were now virtually down and out. They had produced just one real effort on goal, which was headed clear by Ted Hemsley. A mistake by the same player, however, handed possession to City, and after 38 minutes this resulted in a shot by City's Steve Derrett, which, taking a deflection off Trevor Hockey, was diverted past John Hope in the United net to make it 2–1. This fortuitous strike gave renewed heart to the visitors, and in the period preceding half-time they began to impose themselves in midfield and started to cause serious difficulties for the United defence. John Hope, in the thick of the action, went off at the interval with a blood-splattered face after clashing with Alan Warboys.

City's midfield continued to pull the strings in the opening minutes of the second half. Yet the Blades, their team and supporters, remained strong in their belief, and after 55 minutes, having gained a corner, Alan Woodward delivered for Tony Currie to head home and so restore the two-goal lead. It was the defining moment of the match and one of controversy. Currie had risen through a ruck of players and, it was claimed by the City players, had impeded goalkeeper Jim Eadie. Cardiff's manager Jimmy Scoular later claimed that Eadie had 'punched it in after Currie had punched him.' Nevertheless, the goal stood and, after having threatened to make a recovery, City's momentum was lost. United's back four were in complete control. Peter Howard noted that 'Cardiff had nothing to match the calmness of Len Badger and Ted Hemsley; they got little or no change in the air from Eddie Colquhoun and John Flynn.'

Hockey and Currie had now regained control of the midfield, and the endless running of Salmons, Reece and Dearden was pulling City defenders all over the place. After 64 minutes the Blades had their fourth goal as Woodward fed Gil Reece, and the Welshman, who had been rejected by Cardiff as a youngster, exacted sweet revenge by crashing an unstoppable shot past Eadie. With the Lane crowd in ecstasy, the visitors were a spent force. Nine minutes from time Gil Reece slotted a pass to Billy Dearden, who, following a great run, put the ball into the Cardiff net to make it 5–1. United's players had won a crushing, well-deserved victory, and as the final whistle went the players left the field to terrific, emotional acclaim from the throats of thousands of happy fans fully believing their chants of 'We're going up again!'

United's victory had placed them a point clear of Cardiff, should the Welshmen win their game in hand. It had also provided the Blades with a superior goal average, meaning that it was still possible to go up should they not defeat Watford in their final game. Clearly, United were delighted after the match, but it was a delight tempered by a note of caution; the job had yet to be completed and the players had to remain focused on the Watford game coming up on Saturday. Boss John Harris's post-match comments summed up the mood when he said, 'Obviously I was thrilled with last night's performance, but right to the end we shall stick to our policy of treating every match as it comes. We shall plan as

Shattered but happy, United heroes Gil Reece, Billy Dearden and John Flynn relax in the dressing room after the victory against Cardiff.

carefully and with as much determination as was shown last night for Watford. Their win at Cardiff recently showed that they must be treated with respect.'

The mood in South Wales, as to be expected, was one of despondency. *The Western Mail* declared, 'Cardiff can now forget their promotion dreams. Sheffield United looked a promotion side and seem to have reserved their best attacking football for the most critical match of the season.' *The South Wales Echo* added, 'No disputing the validity of United's win. United looked the best side in the division, although there weren't four goals in it.' There was no such acknowledgement of United's prowess from City's manager Jimmy Scoular, however. His comments probably reflected the severe disappointment at the way his club's promotion hopes had seemingly gone, 'Defeat last night was one of the most disappointing moments in my 25 years of football. I feel United's first and third goals were illegal. But good luck to Sheffield United. They should hold their own in the First Division.'

Alan Warboys, Cardiff forward and ex-Wednesday man from nearby Goldthorpe, was left in a state of shock by the result, 'I don't know what happened. This wasn't us tonight. Maybe it was the tension, but the lads are shattered.' Faced with a must-win clash, the Blades had blown their rivals away. Leicester's victory on the same evening at Bristol City had seen the Foxes promoted and now the First Division awaited United. First, however, there was a little matter of Watford.

Match 5

Sheffield United 3–0 Watford
Division Two

1 May 1971

At the end of the season Eddie Colquhoun spoke of the huge pressure that the players had been under during the final run in. It was the weight of expectation that the team should get promotion that proved difficult to bear, but the load had been lightened by the magnificent support that the players had continued to receive from the fans: 'The pressure was fantastic because you had so much faith in us, because you expected so much of us. This was more than offset by the part you all played off the field.' Eddie applauded the fans for keeping the faith, 'Believe me, all the lads will tell you that the encouragement you give us does act as an extra spur, and so does the patience you showed at times when things were not quite going our way.' The players had been inspired by 'the sight of so many fans travelling away to London, Hull and Leicester. You even turned Middlesbrough into a "home" game for us, despite the shocking conditions.' The rapport that the players had with the fans was helped by the close-knit nature of the squad and the fact that they regularly attended supporters' club social evenings together. This probably helped to keep the criticism from becoming too serious when the team hit a difficult patch and performances were poor.

Going into the Watford game, the average attendance at Bramall Lane was 6,000 better than in the last promotion season of 1960–61, while over 100,000 more fans had attended the home games compared to the previous season. It was clear that it was not just the success that had drawn in the fans, but the exciting, attacking brand of football that John

Harris's talented side were delivering on the pitch. The fans were being entertained and they were enjoying it.

Although Harris had given his men a day off following their exertions in Tuesday's victory over Cardiff, several players returned to Bramall Lane on Wednesday for treatment to knocks received in the game. While the players received treatment, John Harris and his assistants, John Short and Cec Coldwell, drove to Watford to see the Hornets' fixture against Swindon. Watford were not a team to be underrated, especially as they had won 1–0 at Ninian Park against Cardiff back on 17 April. As Harris noted, 'Watford have a defensive set up. They try to be strong at the back and break quickly. We might find them difficult to break down. If we do, I know the crowd and the players will be patient. We are ready to climax our nine months of slog and hard work with the result that means everything. Much celebrating has already gone on, but we at the club have not lost sight of the fact that it isn't over yet and Watford won't just come and lie down for us.'

Friday saw Harris, recently announced as the division's Manager of the Month, confidently reveal an unchanged line up for Saturday's fixture. His views that Watford would prove anything but pushovers was underlined by the bullish attitude of Hornets manager Ken Furphy, who was later to manage the Blades. In his pre-match interviews, Furphy declared, 'We have got to be fair to Cardiff. When we beat them away, I told them that we would even things up against Sheffield United. I still think we will win tomorrow. If it is something my players like, it is a big match atmosphere. There is going to be one tomorrow and I am confident. So, sorry Sheffield United, you will just have to sweat it out until Cardiff's result comes through.' Furphy made it clear that he would employ an extra defender and pull back his midfield, with only Stuart Scullion and Tom Walley given any licence to attack. Furphy believed that his team could soak up United's pressure and hit them quickly on the break. Interestingly, besides boss Ken Furphy, other members of the Watford contingent would later find themselves at Bramall Lane: Keith Eddy, Colin Franks, Terry Garbett and Stewart Scullion.

Sheffield United: Hope, Badger, Hemsley, Flynn, Colquhoun, Hockey, Woodward, Salmons, Dearden, Currie, Reece. Substitute: Ford
Watford: Edmunds, Butler, Packer, Franks, Lees, Eddy, Scullion, Garbett, Jennings, Walley, Woods. Substitute: Welbourne
Referee: Mr R.B. Kirkpatrick
Attendance: 38,857

As good as their manager's words, Watford were quick out of the blocks and took the game to United. After eight minutes, the Blades survived a serious shock as Stewart Scullion thumped a shot against United's crossbar. Given a wake-up call that Watford were about to crash the promotion party, the Blades, now driven on by Hockey and Colquhoun, were in no mood to falter. Fortunately, neither the team nor their fans lost their belief and, gradually, the Blades began to overpower their opponents. It was a frantic two-minute spell that finally broke the tension and secured the Blades' victory. In the 21st minute Gil Reece weaved through the Watford defence and, in on goal, was upended in the box by Keith Eddy. From the resulting penalty, Alan Woodward made no mistake to put the Blades in front. Two minutes later Woody repaid the compliment to his fellow forward, playing a great ball into Gil Reece, who smashed it into the corner of the net to make it 2–0.

For the rest of the first half and into the second, Watford valiantly continued their attempts to get back into the game. Scullion and Garbett were showing some clever touches in midfield, and Colin Franks had two goal-bound efforts blocked by Eddie Colquhoun. United's defence, perhaps not surprisingly given the supreme importance of the game, was uncharacteristically nervous and prone to error. Walley, taking advantage of one such moment of confusion, seized hold of a loose ball and advanced on John Hope's goal, only to see his goal-bound shot blocked on the line by Colquhoun. It proved to be Watford's last chance to get back into the game. Only 10 minutes into the second half, however, it was the resurgent Welshman, Gil Reece, rounding off an excellent end to the season for both himself and his team, who scored the third, effectively putting the game beyond the visitors. It was now a matter of continuing to focus and close out the game. Yet with their three-goal lead behind them, the Blades began to play the expansive, attacking

Celebrating promotion in the dressing room following the Watford game. Back row (left to right): Dearden, Reece, Woodward, Currie, Hemsley, Salmons, Hockey, Colquhoun, Flynn, Hope, John Harris and John Short (assistant manager). Front: Cec Coldwell (coach), Ford, Badger.

football that the season had been noted for. In this period they created several chances to extend their lead, but they were unable to capitalise on any of them.

As the game entered its final quarter of an hour, the chants of 'We're going up again!' were echoing all around the ground. As Peter Howard noted, 'The result was an incredible sound, the Lane's own overture for the return of First Division football.'

At the final whistle the celebrations began, the crowd surging on to the pitch and chanting for their heroes. Skipper Eddie Colquhoun and the players emerged in the directors' box in the old John Street stand to take the plaudits.

All the players had proved to be heroes on the day, but perhaps two stood out when the dust finally settled. Gil Reece had scored twice in the crowning achievement of his personal revival. He had regained his place in the team in late January, with manager John Harris providing him with a new roving role up front, rather than his traditional position on the flanks. Reece had responded by rewarding his manager with some superb performances. Billy Dearden was the other; described by *The Star* as 'the lionheart who battled on'. The full extent of the centre-forward's cartilage problems were now out in the open. 'It seems to have locked in nearly every match,' noted Billy, 'but coach Cec Coldwell has been very good at sorting things out during matches, and I've managed to carry on.' On one occasion, while Billy was changing the wheel trims on his car at home, his knee locked and he lay prostrate on the drive for almost an hour before trainer Harry Latham arrived to sort him out!

As congratulations came in from all sides for the Blades, two are worthy of note. Dr Andrew Stephens, chairman of Sheffield Wednesday, reflected a time in which rivalry between the two city sides was not quite as intense – certainly within the clubs' hierarchies – as it is today. Stephens was lavish in his praise for the Blades, telling *The Star* 'I have written to the Blades expressing our admiration and congratulations. Not only have they had a wonderful season, but their performances in the run-in, when the tension was at its greatest, were excellent.' Derek Dooley, future Blades chairman, but then employed at Wednesday, declared, 'I'm sincerely delighted for John Harris's sake. On the occasions I have seen United, they have always impressed.' United chairman Dick Wragg was quick to show similar good feelings towards his neighbours, declaring after the Watford game: 'I'm delighted that United are to bring First Division football back to Sheffield, and I hope Wednesday will join us as soon as possible.'

Harris, however, was already thinking about next season and the serious challenges that lay ahead among football's elite. But before that there was the little matter of the Sheffield and Hallamshire FA County Cup semi-final against Rotherham, to be played on Thursday. So the players were straight back into training on Monday morning. The senior players attended by choice, even though they had been offered a day off by Harris. It was a clear indication of the togetherness of this group of players, which was a key reason why, ultimately, the 1970–71 season had ended in such a successful fashion.

Match 6

Sheffield United 3–0 Leeds United
Division One

17 August 1971

T he visit of Leeds to Bramall Lane was the second fixture of the new season. Optimism among members of the playing squad for United's chances in the campaign ahead had been somewhat dented in pre-season. The team had been well beaten in Holland, 2–0 by Twente Enschede on 6 August. The Blades had been at full strength but were unable to cope with the passing and movement of the Dutchmen. Tony Currie later recalled, 'Twente were a class above us…it seemed as though they had 15 men on the field.' Len Badger remembered that, 'We never touched the ball that day. I thought we were a half decent side, but they were exceptional…they passed us off the park.' On their return to Sheffield, the shocked players held a meeting in which it was acknowledged that they would have to train flat out if they were to survive in the top flight. Peter Howard, writing in the programme for the opening-day fixture against Southampton on 14 August, was more positive about the Dutch experience. He felt that the Twente game: "should have done the Blades some good. Having done so well at the end of last season, it was perhaps as well to be reminded that they are not infallible. Twente performed this important duty well."

On the opening day, the Blades, in a torrential downpour, had proved to be a potent attacking force, defeating Southampton 3–1 with goals from Woodward, Flynn and Salmons. Now, however, the real test had come against Yorkshire-rivals Leeds United. Under Don Revie's guidance, Leeds had become one of the most powerful sides in Europe.

United's opening day match programme proudly announces the club's return to the top flight.

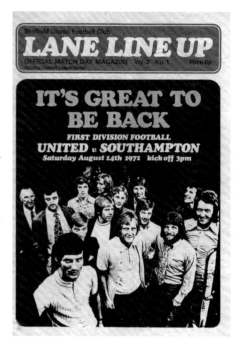

Since 1965 they had twice been beaten FA Cup finalists, had won two Inter-City Fairs Cups, had won the League Championship and had been title runners-up the previous season. Once again Leeds were favourites for the League title and had a squad full of household international names to match. Much of the regional media, especially the Yorkshire TV news programme *Calendar* – or 'Leeds TV' as many Sheffielders called it! – were sure that the new boys from the Lane would be brought down to earth with a bang. They would learn the harsh realities of top-flight football. Leeds would prove too stern a test and a bridge too far for the red-and-white hopefuls.

The Leeds camp were not taking the game lightly, however. The season before United had defeated Leeds 1–0 in the League Cup while still a Second Division side, and Don Revie was known to be a great admirer of the Sheffield club. More recently, Maurice Lindley, Leeds assistant manager, noted after United's victory over Southampton that 'There was flair and imagination and they were far more workmanlike collectively. Obviously, this is an early stage, but I would say they are a better side than any that have gone up for a few seasons.' Yet the Leeds camp were still confident that they would win. Billy Bremner was adamant that his teammates would be far more focused this time around, Leeds' Scottish international skipper declaring, 'Last season when Sheffield beat us in the League Cup we were a bit lacksadaisical; we did not have the usual team talks. But it will be different tomorrow.'

Prior to the game Leeds had slight concerns over Bremner and full-back Terry Cooper, but their biggest doubt was over ex-Blades centre-forward Mick Jones. Jones had been the first United player to be transferred for £100,000 at the start of the relegation season of 1967–68, and he was eager to play against his former team. Jones was carrying a groin strain from a pre-season friendly against Morton, however, and had missed the opening game at Maine Road against Manchester City.

The Blades expected to field the same side as they had against Southampton, the only possible change being if Gil Reece had recovered from a badly-gashed leg to challenge new signing Stewart Scullion's place in the side. John Harris was anticipating a tough encounter, declaring, 'Leeds are the finest team in the country, bar none. We know that we've got a fight on our hands and if we do as well as last year we'll be delighted.' Harris sent a rallying cry out to the fans asking them for 'another night like Cardiff'.

Sheffield United: Hope, Badger, Hemsley, Flynn, Colquhoun, Hockey, Woodward, Salmons, Dearden, Currie, Scullion. Substitute: Ford
Leeds United: Sprake, Reaney, Madeley, Bremner, Charlton, Hunter, Lorimer, Clarke, Belfitt, Giles, Bates. Substitute: Yorath
Referee: Mr W.S. Castle
Attendance: 40,725

United's line up was indeed unchanged, while Leeds saw changes at left-back with Cooper, still injured, replaced by Paul Madeley, and Rod Belfitt continued to deputise for Jones. Mick Bates was drafted in to fill the gap left by Madeley's switch back into the defence.

It was a tight first half as the Blades tried hard to raise the tempo and put the visitors under the heavy attacking pressure that had caused Southampton such discomfort in their previous home game. Leeds, however, proved to be a much tougher proposition. With a back five that boasted five internationals, and fronted by a central midfield that contained the tough-tackling duo of Billy Bremner and Norman Hunter, the Blades were finding it difficult to make any impression on the Leeds goal. In typically belligerent fashion, United's Trevor Hockey was trying his best to unsettle his midfield opponents. His strenuous efforts, however, led to his entry into referee Castle's notebook, joined in the first half by Hunter. As half-time approached, United began to assert themselves and their main strength was coming from the precocious midfield talent Tony Currie, ably supported on the right flank by Alan Woodward.

As the second half got under way it was Currie who began to pull the strings, running with and using the ball to great effect, as he looked to put Billy Dearden in behind the Leeds defence and feed Woodward on the right. Producing some purposeful runs and crosses, 'Woody' was proving particularly devastating with the delivery of his corners. The pressure that the Blades were putting on Gary Sprake and the Leeds defence from these set pieces meant that the Welsh 'keeper was finding it difficult to punch the ball away or take it cleanly. In the 55th minute, Dearden, receiving the ball, ran at the Leeds defence, only for the ball to be cleared for another corner on the right at the Bramall Lane end. 'Woody' sent in yet another inswinger that eluded the grasp of Sprake, and this time John Flynn, moving in behind Jack Charlton, rose at the far post to head the ball between Bremner and Paul Reaney, waiting to clear on the goal line, and into the net. The Blades had gone a goal up amidst ecstatic scenes of jubilation from the massed ranks of their fans.

The goal, however, provided a real wake-up call for the visitors, who now began to mount a series of their own attacks. After 62 minutes, a mistake by Ted Hemsley on

Leeds 'keeper Gary Sprake is in 'no-mans land' as John Flynn rises to head United into the lead.

United's left let in Peter Lorimer, who advanced into the box and rounded Blades 'keeper John Hope who, flailing at Lorimer's feet, seemed to bring down the Scottish international. The Leeds players made strong appeals for a penalty, but they were turned down by referee Castle, who continue to ignore their ongoing complaints. As the pressure increased, the match became more fractious, but the Blades continued to hold out as the visitors' efforts went narrowly wide. With just over five minutes to go, a Jack Charlton shot was charged down in the United box to a chorus of Leeds demands for handball and a penalty. Again, the referee waved away the appeals, and the mood of all the players was not helped by the resultant mêlée of Leeds players around the harassed official as they demanded that he reconsider his decision.

As the tension mounted, Lorimer fouled Currie, leading to an altercation between both sets of players. With Leeds desperate for an equaliser and still smarting from their failure to grab a penalty, the inevitable happened. Scullion picked up a loose ball and raced away down the left. Committed to attack, Leeds had left themselves wide open at the back. Scullion's quick break was responded to by Geoff Salmons and Billy Dearden, both of whom raced down the centre of the pitch. Scullion, near the byline, played in a great low ball across the Leeds area which, eluding Sprake and the retreating Reaney, found its way to Dearden, who squeezed in the ball from a narrow angle at the far post to make it 2–0 and send the Blades fans into raptures. With just minutes left it seemed to be all over for Leeds, and two minutes later it was. Breaking on the counter-attack, United won yet another corner on the Leeds right. Again, Woodward delivered to the far post and John Flynn, out jumping the Leeds defence, knocked the ball back across goal for his central-defensive partner Eddie Colquhoun to head home.

To say that the crowd went wild was an understatement. It was an outpouring of emotions, of pride in the city at a time when Leeds had been such a dominant footballing force, of hope that United were now reasserting themselves after having been belittled by the regional media at the expense of their Yorkshire rivals. The previous season's Cup win had been no flash in the pan; Leeds were no longer the great masters and United had beaten them again.

The Blades had made a fantastic start to their First Division campaign and the team had shown more than enough ability and determination to suggest that they could achieve more than mere survival. But the points had been gained in front of the Bramall Lane faithful. The key question now was whether they would fare so well when they travelled to Everton and Arsenal for their next fixtures: clubs which had been League champions in the previous two seasons.

Match 7

Arsenal 0–1 Sheffield United
Division One

24 August 1971

With two home wins to start the season, United travelled to face Everton at Goodison Park in an optimistic mood. In front of another large crowd of over 40,000, United again came out on top. Defensively solid, with Flynn and Colquhoun outstanding in the centre of defence, the Blades, in a tight game, gradually found opportunities opening up in the Everton defence as the game entered its final quarter. With 10 minutes to go, Alan Woodward broke away and, after a run of 30 yards, smashed one of his unstoppable specials into the right-hand upper corner of the Everton net. So United, with six points out of six, had the only 100 per cent record in Division One and sat proudly at top of the table. Even Everton boss Harry Catterick, formerly manager of Sheffield Wednesday, had to reverse his previous pessimistic assessments of United's ability to compete in the top flight. Catterick declared in his after-match comments, 'After this I think they'll do well. I thought they were very tight and they worked hard for each other.'

And so it was on to face the current double winners, the mighty Arsenal, for a Wednesday night fixture at Highbury. The Gunners had won two of their opening three games and were sat two points behind the Blades in the early First Division table. Manchester United's victory over West Bromwich Albion 24 hours earlier had taken them a point above the Blades, who were now looking to restore their position at the top of the table.

Arsenal: Wilson, Rice, McNab, Storey, McLintock, Simpson, Armstrong, Kelly, Radford, Kennedy, Graham. Substitute: Roberts
Sheffield United: Hope, Badger, Hemsley, Flynn, Colquhoun, Hockey, Woodward, Salmons, Dearden, Currie, Scullion. Substitute: Barlow
Referee: Mr J. Hunting
Attendance: 45,339

United, unchanged for the fourth successive game, set off with real purpose, and after just five minutes they stunned the huge Highbury crowd by taking the lead. Typical of United's football to date, the goal was another example of their attacking flair. A flowing move began with Len Badger, in his own half, passing the ball out to Ted Hemsley, who fed Billy Dearden down the left. Dearden moved the ball on to Geoff Salmons, who whipped around right-back Pat Rice and crossed the ball into the Arsenal box. 'Keeper Bob Wilson blocked Woodward's resulting shot, but the ball ran loose and Stewart Scullion scampered in to knock the ball home for his first goal for the club. As the *Sheffield Telegraph*'s reporter Bill Thornton noted, 'It was a brilliantly engineered goal, stamped with the flair that is becoming United's trademark and which is already causing a tremour to run through First Division camps up and down the country.'

Arsenal had no response as the Blades continued to dominate the game. Geoff Salmons and Tony Currie were breaking dangerously from midfield and feeding Scullion and Woodward on the left and right flanks, while Billy Dearden was roving through the middle. The United forwards were mercilessly pulling apart the Arsenal defence. During a frantic three-minute spell, the Blades should have put the game well beyond doubt. After 26 minutes, Woodward, put clear by a great ball from Salmons, fired over with the goal at his mercy. Tony Currie then tricked his way past Arsenal's Peter Storey and sent in a delicious ball, which Dearden was not quite able to get enough contact on to beat Wilson. Billy then raced on to a pass by Scullion and sent in a terrific low shot, only to see goalkeeper Bob Wilson pull off a great save. Still the Blades were not finished, and after 35 minutes a teasing free-kick was headed just inches over the bar by John Flynn with Wilson well beaten. United's central-defender was proving a real aerial danger to the Gunners' defence at set pieces, just like in previous games.

United were well on top as the half ended, but only had the one goal to show for it. Against a side of Arsenal's undoubted quality, it seemed likely that the Gunners would recover, and so it proved as the second period got underway. Arsenal manager Bertie Mee must have provided an inspired half-time team talk because his players, sensing the danger of their position, flew out of the traps. Seven minutes in, the Arsenal crowd exploded into life as Simpson rose to head in Armstrong's corner. The cheers were soon muted, however, as referee Mr Hunting ruled that United's 'keeper John Hope had been pushed in the back

'Red hot', the magical 'TC' weaves his way through the Everton defence prior to the game at Arsenal.

and so disallowed the goal. Testing the resolve of United's central-defensive pairing of John Flynn and Eddie Colquhoun, Arsenal pursued the tactic of feeding their wide man, George Armstrong, who sent in a succession of testing high crosses into the United area with the aim of hitting the heads of big men John Radford and Ray Kennedy. United stayed strong, however, and young John Hope was in outstanding form as he thwarted two almost certain Arsenal strikes within a minute. He tipped a bending, dipping shot around the post and then followed with a point-blank block from a McLintock shot, rushing out to smother the ball as it rebounded to Graham's feet.

Solid at the back, United proved dangerous on the break, and near the end almost made it two as Currie twisted and turned past McLintock in the box, only to see Wilson keep the ball out with his legs. The incident was a sign of the growing stature of 'TC'. Having now played against the finest midfields in the country in his last three games, Currie had dominated. As the newspapers began to realise, not embarrassed to spare the puns, the young midfielder was indeed 'red hot Currie'! John Harris had clearly unearthed a real gem when signing the player from Watford in United's relegation season. The whole country now realised what a great player in the making the Blades had in their ranks.

Given Arsenal's status as double winners and the fact that United had now successfully defeated the last three League champions, this result was the one that really made the national press sit up and take notice. The general mood was summed up in the *Daily Express* headline of 25 August, which declared, 'Call them Sheffield the magnificent!' Assessing United's performance, the *Express* was effusive in its praise for 'these almost anonymous heroes who top the First Division.' 'Anonymous' was a reference to the fact that United's team included Billy Dearden from Chester, Stewart Scullion from Watford, John Flynn from Workington, Ted Hemsley from Shrewsbury and Geoff Salmons and John Hope, who had played just a handful of First Division games.

Analysing the Arsenal game, the *Express* declared, 'Arsenal can find no alibis to take away the glory and superb performance of Sheffield United. And it was as simple as this. Sheffield were "United" and a far better team than Arsenal. They played a simple game magnificently. They played it with confidence, a glowing spirit and incredible stamina. Sheffield played so tremendously well that they were warmly saluted by the Arsenal players and cheered by the Arsenal crowd. Arsenal were beaten by one of the best teams I've seen for many a season.'

The Daily Mirror's headline noted, 'Arsenal's first home defeat for 28 matches' and their article went on, 'Arsenal were driven to despair last night by the skill and common sense that has shot Sheffield United to the top of the First Division…their victory was no fluke. They arrived back from the Second Division this season and it is no accident which finds them leading the first.'

United's chief coach, Cec Coldwell, attributed his team's current success to the foundation of 'selfless running…disciplined organisation…[and] team spirit second to none.' It was this that had allowed their attacking flair to thrive and all Blades fans hoped that it would long continue.

Manchester United 2–0 Sheffield United Division One

2 October 1971

When the Blades visited Old Trafford they were on a 22-match unbeaten run stretching back to their promotion drive in Division Two. Currently, they were 10 games undefeated in the top flight, which was the best start by any team to a Division One season for many years. The Blades had enjoyed four wins and two draws in their six home games, while they had won all their away games so far. To add to the victories at Everton and Arsenal, the Blades had won 3–2 at Nottingham Forest and 1–0 at Leicester. In their last game on 25 September, they had defeated Chelsea 1–0 at Bramall Lane.

The plaudits for the Blades continued to come. The *Forest Review* on United's victorious visit to the City Ground on 4 September declared, 'Come next May, the championship may well not go to Bramall Lane, despite their fine start, but at least they have shown in the early matches that good football is still a very effective weapon in the armoury of those who prefer to rely on skill in attack, rather than defensive ploys that often make watching and playing the game a somewhat tedious occupation.' Ken Huston writing in *Inside Football* noted, 'Sheffield United have brought a breath of fresh air into Division One, that bastion of defensive soccer. The critics said that their free-flowing, open style was alright in the Second Division, but did not stand much chance of succeeding against the crack defences of the top table. But, so far, United have succeeded in showing that the best method of defence is attack.'

Keep Fit
The United Way

Members of the Lane Social Club can now enjoy the use of the players'

SAUNA BATH
and Keep Fit equipment
OPENING ON 4th OCTOBER, 1971

Single **60p**
13 weeks' season ticket, 1 per week
£5.85

Apply to Lane Social Club or Pools Office

Men:
Monday, Wednesday and Friday, 1.0-10.0 p.m.
Women: Tuesday and Thursday, 1.0-10.0 p.m.

"We are United"

United fans are offered the opportunity to use the players' new sauna in the match programme against Chelsea.

United's start had certainly stunned the football world. When the Blades visited Leicester on 18 September, the Foxes' programme declared, 'The $64,000 question every Saturday evening is – have Sheffield United been beaten yet? The soccer world has looked on in disbelieving admiration as, week by week, they cast aside the most distinguished of opponents.'

One of the reasons for the Blades' continued success, believed manager John Harris, was 'the vociferous and enthusiastic encouragement of our supporters'. The Blades boss explained that, 'At the Nottingham and Leicester matches we knew we had vast numbers of our fans cheering our team on. The lads knew it and it made all the difference. Quite honestly, it was almost like playing at home, so great was the encouragement given and, naturally, the players responded.' United's success had gained John Harris the Bells Whiskey Manager of the Month award for August, while the performances of Alan Woodward saw his selection by Sir Alf Ramsey for the Football League XI versus the Irish League XI in Dublin, and Gil Reece, Trevor Hockey and Eddie Colquhoun were selected for the Welsh and upcoming Scottish squads respectively. Blades fans were also rewarded by the continuing transformation of the Pavilion, and members of the Lane Social Club were now able to enjoy the use of the players' sauna bath for a cost of 60p a session or £5.85 for a 13-week season ticket. The new Lane restaurant had also opened its doors at the end of September.

A key factor in Sheffield United's success, believed Manchester United boss Frank O' Farrell, writing in the Old Trafford programme, was that the Blades had 'been lucky with injuries and, with the right results coming steadily for them, they have been able to field a virtually unchanged team throughout the season so far.' With Eddie Colquhoun passing a late fitness test, the Blades were again to be unchanged for the 12th successive League and Cup game.

The match at Old Trafford was pitching the now-legendary team from the Lane against a surprisingly resurgent Manchester United side. The game aroused huge interest, not only on both sides of the Pennines but across the country as a whole, reflected by the presence of the *Match of the Day* television cameras. Many commentators felt that the Manchester United team contained too many players who had seen their best days – Bobby Charlton, Denis Law, Tony Dunne, John Sadler, Alex Stepney – and a period of redevelopment and restructuring was essential. Yet the Red Devils' start to the season was almost as spectacular as that of the Blades. Drawing two and winning three of their first five games, despite being forced to play their first two home games on neutral ground against Arsenal at Liverpool and West Brom at Stoke, due to crowd trouble. Therefore, their start had been solid, yet having been beaten 1–0 by Everton on 31 August, assumptions were made that Manchester United's form would now take a turn for the worse. The opposite actually occurred as they won their next three League games and, prior to facing the Blades, achieved an excellent draw against a powerful Liverpool side at Anfield. The First Division table thus saw Manchester United in second place after 10 games, three points behind the Blades.

Victory for the White Rose would see the Blades stretch their lead to five points over the Lancastrians and, as a result, Sheffield United's chief coach Cec Coldwell, interviewed on the eve of the match, believed that 'they may be under more pressure than us, especially as they are at home.' Given that Manchester United's boss Frank O'Farrell had managed Leicester to promotion prior to moving to Old Trafford at the start of the season, he was well aware of Sheffield United's qualities and, unlike others, was not about to underestimate them. O'Farrell had his team ready and prepared. The clash of the top two was about to begin.

The fantastic interest in the game suggested it would be a full house, but no one could have predicted the record numbers swarming around the Old Trafford ground well before three o'clock. Arriving 70 minutes before kick-off, Sheffield United's players and officials had to leave their coach and force their way through a closely-packed crowd for the last 40 yards to enter the official Old Trafford entrance. Travel was equally difficult for the thousands of fans from Sheffield. The 10:05 train from the Midland station should have arrived at Manchester Piccadilly an hour later, but a broken train on the line meant that it did not reach there until 12:35. The first 'football special' train, leaving at 11:50, was to contain many Blades fans who failed to secure entry as gates closed at 2.20pm, and an estimated 20,000 fans remained locked outside, unable to gain entry to the terraces by paying on the turnstile. Tickets for seats had been available prior to the match but had sold out well in advance. This did not stop ticket touts from acquiring them and selling them on for seven times their face value, such was the desire to see the game. The police were effectively overwhelmed and there were announcements for fans to go home, but these were ignored as some supporters, on both sides, tried to climb over the walls or force the gates. Most stayed outside the ground to listen to their transistor radios as the Radio Two sports programme was carrying a full commentary on the game. Given the non-segregation of fans, and the tense and confused circumstances, it is perhaps surprising that only one serious incident was reported between rival fans. It was fantastic for the Blades that over 70,000 had turned up to see them and that the club was in the national limelight. It was now hoped that the team would put the icing on the cake by achieving a memorable victory.

Manchester United: Stepney, O'Neill, Dunne, Gowling, James, Sadler, Morgan, Kidd, Charlton, Best, Aston. Substitute: Burns

Sheffield United: Hope, Badger, Hemsley, Flynn, Colquhoun, Hockey, Woodward, Salmons, Dearden, Currie, Scullion. Substitute: Reece, replacing Hemsley

Referee: Mr K.E. Walker

Attendance: 51,735

Although it was early October, the game was played in hot, sunny conditions, making the strenuous efforts of both sets of players particularly impressive. As previously noted, the Blades were unchanged, although Eddie Colquhoun was wearing strapping to his thigh. The Red Devils, however, were forced into a late change as Denis Law had been injured in Friday's training session, and John Aston came into a rearranged attacking line up.

It was the Blades who, in a fantastic atmosphere, added to by the enthusiastic thousands from Sheffield, threatened first, quickly gaining a corner, after which Ted Hemsley fired over the bar following a free-kick. Fiercely competitive from the start, the home side soon responded, a great ball from Dunne almost reaching George Best in the box, only for Trevor Hockey to clear the ball for a corner. Len Badger then sent Tony Currie away and his shot was expertly tipped over the bar by Alex Stepney. At the other end, the increasingly influential Alan Gowling produced a strong run and a shot that beat a despairing John Hope, but the ball rolled inches wide of the far post.

It was Stewart Scullion, rising to the challenge of the Old Trafford stage, who was most prominent in the Sheffield attack. 'His Scottish craft must have amazed the Manchester United fans, attuned as they are to seeing only the best,' declared the *Telegraph*'s Benny Hill. His brilliant running and skill with the ball was creating huge problems for the Reds' defence. Yet Tony Currie, not far behind Scullion, reminded everyone of his quality as he burst through and powered in a long-range drive, which only just dipped over Stepney's crossbar.

The Blades defence and midfield, tight and compact, were doing a brilliant job to contain the attacking threat of the talented Reds forward line, in particular George Best. The Irishman reminded everyone of the threat that he posed, however, when a brilliant ball from Bobby Charlton opened up a square Sheffield defence and, but for the alertness of 'keeper John Hope, scrambling out to smother the ball, Best, racing through, would surely have scored. As half-time approached though, the Reds had Stepney to thank for keeping them level, as Badger's quickly-taken free-kick released Scullion, who, through on goal, was denied by the Manchester 'keeper, who came out brilliantly to dive at the Scotsman's feet and block an almost certain goal.

Level at half-time, the Blades certainly created more and better chances than their opponents and emerged for the second half to a rapturous ovation from the huge Blades following located all around the Old Trafford ground. Conceding an early free-kick for Flynn's foul on Best, the Blades were momentarily on the back foot. A surging run from Geoff Salmons, however, weaving his way up and across the pitch from 25 yards inside his own half, and ending with a shot wide of the post, re-established Sheffield United's attacking menace. Currie then burst down the right, cut inside from the edge of the area and fired in a shot that was saved well by Stepney at the foot of his near post.

Given the potency of both teams' attacks, the absence of goals up to this point was somewhat surprising, and again it seemed that the Blades were most likely to break the deadlock. While Stepney had been forced into several fine saves, John Hope had had none of any real difficulty. Alan Woodward then raced down the right and put over a dangerous cross that was taken well by Stepney, who was then enormously relieved to see a fierce right foot shot from Scullion fly across the face of his goal, with Dearden narrowly failing to apply the finishing touch. Stepney then saved a good long-range effort from Dearden, the Blades centre-forward, following this up with a great run down the left, pulling the ball across for Scullion who, mistiming his effort, failed to convert a good chance.

With 12 minutes to go, the Blades lost left-back Ted Hemsley with an ankle injury, with Gil Reece – a forward – replacing him and causing a reshuffle of the Blades side. Most likely, although we can never really know, Hemsley's loss on the left of the defence was significant in the game's defining moment, which took place with just six minutes left. George Best, receiving the ball just over the halfway line, drifted from left to right across the Sheffield defence and, going past four players, accelerated and brilliantly twisted the ball back across goal from a narrow angle to beat Hope's despairing dive for the ball to go in off the far post to the delight of the home support. It was a brilliant goal, stamped with the hallmark of Best's genius, and one that has haunted Blades fans down the years as it has been re-run time after time on television. Yet, if Ted Hemsley had still been on the pitch, who knows…?

With the Blades desperately trying to get on level terms and throwing men forward, Gowling fed Brian Kidd, who raced away down the left and delivered a superb cross into the middle, where Alan Gowling, having raced down the pitch in support, finished it off with a superb header to make it 2–0 and game over. It was Sheffield United's first defeat since being beaten the previous season by Hull City, an impressive 23 games ago.

Although the Blades had lost, they were still a point clear at the top of the First Division, and there was determination that their challenge at the top should continue. After all, the team had played well and, on balance, deserved to get something from the game. John

Harris was bitterly disappointed. Acknowledging the genius of Best's strike, he still insisted that his team had the opportunities to have won the game well before then, 'It was a great goal. I didn't think there was any danger when he picked up the ball, but, anyway, by that time we could, and should, have been in the lead.' Captain Eddie Colquhoun did not feel that the Blades had played as well as at other times during the season, declaring, 'We worked hard as usual, but I thought we lacked a bit of flair and imagination.' Reds boss O'Farrell, also noting that the genius of George Best had turned the game, agreed that the Blades had not really deserved to lose, declaring, 'United took a lot of beating today and they are obviously on top of Division One on merit. They deserve to be where they are.'

To rally his beaten side, Harris issued them a challenge, 'Now we have got to keep at it and try and retain the consistency shown in our long stretch without defeat.' But would the team be able to respond?

Sheffield United 7–0 Ipswich Town Division One

27 November 1971

John Harris's desire for United to go on another undefeated run to maintain their position at the top of the table was, unfortunately, not realised. The confidence gained from their blistering start to the season was seriously undermined by a four-run losing streak in the League, which began at Old Trafford and was followed up by a 3–2 home defeat to Stoke and away reversals at Southampton 3–2 and Manchester City 2–1. The rot was put to an end with a battling goalless draw at Arsenal in the League Cup fourth round on 26 October, followed at home by a 1–1 draw against Liverpool on 30 October, where a crowd of 39,023 saw Tony Currie smash a magnificent 40-yard shot past Ray Clemence.

The Star's Peter Howard, writing in his regular column in United's programme for the game against Liverpool, tried to analyse just why the Blades had entered on 'a disturbing run which has seen them slip from leading the League by three points to trailing overtakers Manchester United by five points.' He was dismissive of the cynics who argued that United's early form had been a fluke. The players had 'set themselves a remarkably high standard at the outset, the longer it went on the harder it was bound to become.' Howard believed that 'the problems now facing the Blades are mainly in the mind'. Perhaps, however, there was a point he was missing. United had a relatively small squad of top-quality players, and there was not the flexibility for Harris to significantly change the side in light of losses in form, niggling injuries or tiredness. Young players Steve Cammack, Steve Goulding, Ian Holmes, Alan Ogden and Ian Mackenzie were all to play later during the season, but none were of the standard sufficient to cover for the able first-choice members of the squad. Those seasoned professionals who could be brought in were small in number, effectively only numbering Frank Barlow, David Ford and Gil Reece, and, of these three, arguably Reece was the only player of true quality.

Following the Arsenal and Liverpool games, United seemed to be recovering their form with a 2–1 away victory at West Ham in the League, a 2–0 triumph over Arsenal in their League Cup replay at Bramall Lane and a home victory, also 2–0, against Coventry on 13 November. Yet inconsistency was creeping in and the Blades, beaten 5–0 by West Ham, were disastrously knocked out of the League Cup at the quarter-final stage, before they were beaten 3–0 by the eventual League champions Derby County at the Baseball Ground. Although United's away performances had not been as bad as the scorelines suggested, having slipped to fifth in the division the Blades welcomed Bobby Robson's Ipswich Town to the Lane on Saturday 27 November with a point to prove.

Ipswich were likely to prove difficult opponents. Placed 12th in the table, five points behind the Blades, they were a solid, if not spectacular First Division outfit and had some good players: Laurie Sivell, although only 5ft 8in, had proved to be a top-class 'keeper, young Mick Mills at right-back would later become an England stalwart, South African Colin Viljoen was a hard-working and accomplished midfielder, Allan Hunter was a solid centre-half and Northern Ireland international. Bobby Robson had also recently signed striker Rod Belfitt from Leeds for £50,000 and he had scored in his first two games. Most familiar to the Blades fans was Mick Hill, who, back in 1967, had taken over as United centre-forward when England international Mick Jones departed for Leeds. Hill had made a total of 38 League and Cup appearances for the Blades, scoring 10 goals before moving to Ipswich in October 1969. Ipswich came to the Lane with the second-best defensive record in the League. The stage was, therefore, set for an intriguing match.

Sheffield United: Hope, Badger, Hemsley, Flynn, Hockey, Woodward, Salmons, Dearden, Currie, Reece. Substitute: Scullion
Ipswich Town: Sivell, Hammond, Harper, Viljoen, Hunter, Jefferson, Robertson, Collard, Belfitt, Hill, Miller. Substitute: Clarke, replacing Hill
Referee: Mr W. J. Gow
Attendance: 26,231

With steady rain before kick-off and the Yorkshire television cameras present, Ipswich were forced into one change, with an injury to Mick Mills bringing Jeff Hammond in at right-back. United had Billy Dearden back at centre-forward after an absence of six games. Gil Reece, his replacement, moved out to the left with Stewart Scullion dropping to the bench.

Chosen to represent Wales and Scotland respectively, Trevor Hockey and Eddie Colquhoun add their names to the honours board in the Lane Social Club.

Given their recent form, it was not surprising that the Blades, kicking towards the Shoreham Street end, started nervously. Yet, after five minutes, a great run by Geoff Salmons led to a shot from Alan Woodward, which Ipswich's captain Derek Jefferson scrambled off the line. A minute later, the Blades were again close to taking the lead as Gil Reece headed Woodward's corner beyond 'keeper Laurie Sivell, only to see Allan Hunter knock the ball off the line. Living dangerously, Ipswich were unable to stop United from taking the lead after just nine minutes. The move started with a pass from Ted Hemsley down the left to Billy Dearden, who passed out wide to Alan Woodward, who, cutting inside, shot the ball beyond Sivell's despairing dive and inside the left-hand post.

Yet for the next 20 minutes the visitors really came into the game and, in the words of the *Telegraph*'s Martin Leach, 'contributed notably to a frenetic period, while an edgy United searched for pattern and rhythm and, at times, barely survived at the back.' With Colin Viljoen finding lots of space in midfield, the South African was prompting some dangerous attacks and twice had the opportunity to equalise himself. His first shot was scrambled away by 'keeper John Hope, his second hooked off the line by Eddie Colquhoun. John Flynn was then booked after 18 minutes when he hauled back Mick Hill, who was in on goal. Yet United also had their own opportunities, most notably when Currie's great pass carved open the Ipswich defence, and Dearden's run on goal was only halted by Sivell brilliantly diving at the centre-forward's feet at the edge of the box.

With the game finely balanced after half an hour, the Blades turned the match on its head, going on to devastate the visitors with a three-goal burst in just five minutes. The first came from the penalty spot courtesy of Alan Woodward, following Allan Hunter's scything tackle that felled the flying Geoff Salmons just inside the box. Three minutes later, from a United corner, a cleverly-worked set play saw Woodward send in a pinpoint cross, and Gil Reece, having lost his marker, glanced a superb header past Sivell to make it 3–0. Two minutes later, the normally reliable Sivell was at fault as Len Badger sent in a speculative 30-yard shot, which squirmed through the unhappy 'keeper's hands and into the net for 4–0. Devastated by United's goal blitz, there seemed no way back for the visitors. At half-time it was not only Ipswich who were in need of urgent help and recovery as the goal at the Shoreham Street end of the ground needed emergency repairs!

After half-time United were simply irresistible, determined not to take their foot off the pedal and keen to reward their fans with a brilliant performance. After 15 minutes the Blades were five goals up. Salmons took a throw-in to Trevor Hockey, who fed Gil Reece, whose clever flick into the centre was prodded home by Billy Dearden on his return to the side. Shortly after, a slip by Jefferson was seized upon by Hockey who, bursting through on Sivell's goal, drove his shot just wide of the post. The let off for Ipswich proved temporary, however, as the best goal of the game came after 57 minutes, when a great long ball from Hockey was thumped home on the volley by Alan Woodward for his hat-trick goal and United's sixth.

To their credit, although overwhelmed by United's incisive attacking football, the visitors did not give in, with Miller, Hill and Viljoen all producing good efforts on the United goal. Ex-Blade Mick Hill was substituted by boss Bobby Robson after 66 minutes, replaced by Frank Clarke, leaving the field to a round of applause from the crowd. Substitute Clarke almost reduced the deficit, but it was clearly not Ipswich's day, as when he slipped the ball past John Hope, Flynn was chasing back to clear the ball off the line. With 10 minutes to go, the Blades rounded off the scoring as Geoff Salmons fired in a fierce drive that Sivell could only parry and Woodward blasted the rebound into the net. It was the first time that United had scored seven since beating Swansea 7–1 on 20 December 1952, although that result had been in Division Two.

Following their devastating three-goal burst in five minutes during the first half, United had put on a confident performance and had shown the irresistible form seen at the beginning of the season. So impressive were they that Ipswich boss Bobby Robson declared, 'I thought there were about 17 players in red-and-white shirts out there!' Interviewed after the game, match hero Alan Woodward – the first Blade to score four goals in a League game since Derek 'Doc' Pace against Charlton on 20 December 1958 – acknowledged that 'in the first half hour we were a bit edgy,' but after that, 'I don't think anyone could hold us when we were in that form.' Ipswich striker Mick Hill was full of admiration for the Blades and their performance, declaring, 'They must be the best team we've faced. We've played what we thought were the best and held them, but for United to score seven is something else.'

Yet United were to become a real Jekyll and Hyde team as a week later, this time in front of the BBC's *Match of the Day* cameras, another horror story unfolded as the Blades crashed 5–1 to the division's bottom club Crystal Palace at Selhurst Park. A season that promised so much was starting to become frustrating. Following the Palace result, United seemed to be recovering their best form again and went unbeaten in their next five League games. A home FA Cup third-round defeat to Second Division Cardiff, on 15 January 1972, by three goals to one was hugely disappointing. Blades fans had felt that as United, at their best, could beat anyone in the country, the FA Cup offered a real chance of success. Defeat to the team so emphatically overpowered for promotion back in April was a shock, and the optimism of the fans received another huge setback when the team crashed 5–0 at home to Arsenal two weeks later, made worse by Alan Ball rubbing in the Londoners' superiority by cheekily sitting on the ball during play. The remainder of the season saw the Blades settle into a mid-table position, eventually finishing 10th, which, but for their phenomenal start to the season, would have been regarded as an excellent achievement following on from their recent promotion.

Match 10

Bristol Rovers 0–0 Sheffield United
Watney Cup Final

(Bristol Rovers won 7–6 on penalties)
5 August 1972

The Watney Cup is important in the history of English football, given that it was the first competition to receive sponsorship. Prior to the competition's introduction as a pre-season tournament in August 1970, Allan Hardaker, the outspoken secretary of the Football League, declared, 'The Football League would never be a party to cheap advertising exercises. If industry wishes to tie itself to Britain's number-one sport through the medium of the Football League, it must do so on the understanding that a measure of restraint, indeed decorum, is necessary on both sides.' Given that today's football cannot possibly survive on gate receipts, souvenir sales and club fundraising activities alone, and that commercial sponsorship is such a huge part of the game's finances, it is perhaps surprising to us that there was a great deal of entrenched opposition to sponsorship in the football world prior to the start of the 1970s.

In that less commercial era, many had felt that sponsorship would detract from the image of the game and threaten its dignity. The need for fresh injections of money into the game was clear, however, and, in a sense, the Watney Cup was almost a pilot scheme to test the impact that sponsorship would have on the professional game. Given the concerns of administrators like Hardaker, it is not surprising that negotiations had carried on tentatively for two years before the proposed new competition was firmed up and ready to go in August 1970. Brewers Watney were considered a 'responsible commercial organisation', and it was hoped that their competition would encourage the open, attacking style of football that would be attractive to supporters and strengthen the health and popularity of the game.

The competition involved the top two scoring teams of each of the four divisions, once the promoted teams and those who had qualified for Europe were taken out. The First Division sides were to play those from the Third, the Second those from the Fourth. The top scoring team would be at home and play would be on a straight knockout basis, with the winners having to play three games. Another key innovation of the competition was that if any game were level after 90 minutes, or extra-time if played, a penalty shoot-out would commence. Each side would select five players and the teams would take their penalties in turn, one at a time. If both teams were level after this, sudden death would then ensue. This system was, of course, later adopted by UEFA and FIFA for the European and World Cup competitions.

United, as the top scorers in Division Two, had participated in the inaugural competition, defeating Fourth Division Aldershot 6–0 away before losing 1–0 in the semi-final to the eventual winners, First Division Derby County. The Blades had been pleased with their participation in the competition, given that it had provided a more intensive edge to their pre-season preparations, much better than the usual workout given to the players in friendlies. The club programme for the first home game of the season against Swindon on 22 August 1970 declared the ties 'far better for getting settled in than friendly games, owing to the spirit in which they were played.'

Promoted in 1970–71, the Blades were not eligible for the competition. In 1972, however, as one of the top First Division scorers on their return to the top flight, they qualified again for the Watney Cup. The fact that the BBC broadcasted highlights of all three rounds of the tournament showed that there was great interest in these games. United coasted through 3–0 against Third Division Notts County at Meadow Lane on 29 July – a notable highlight being an Alan Woodward thunderbolt that flashed past the post and knocked out a supporter behind the goal. The Blades then defeated Fourth Division Peterborough 4–0 at London Road, setting up the Final against Third Division Bristol Rovers at Eastville. Healthy crowds of 14,405, 9,207 and 19,768 respectively for United's fixtures indicate the enthusiasm of the lower-division clubs' supporters; the competition was so popular mainly due to the fact that it gave them the opportunity to play against top-flight sides and provided opportunities for some giant killing.

Bristol Rovers had reached the Final by defeating First Division Wolves, followed by Second Division Burnley in the semi-final. Rovers had scored four times without reply and had clearly proved tough opponents. Managing the Pirates was former Sheffield Wednesday captain Don Megson. Megson was clearly enthused by the prospect of playing the Blades, 'Regardless of the opposition, we would go out with only success in mind, but with United here it makes it rather special. The Wednesday versus United atmosphere never leaves you when you have been brought up in it.' Megson was also bullish about his side's prospects, saying 'We will play our normal way, which is to attack. Certainly I think we can win. United are a fine side, but as our results against Wolves and Burnley showed, so are we.'

Both sides were unchanged for the game. For United, Len Badger, injured in the first game against Notts County, was still absent, replaced by Steve Goulding. Their new £50,000 signing from Watford, Keith Eddy, was on the bench. Tony Currie, sent off against Peterborough in the semi-final, was facing an automatic three-match suspension under the new 'get tough' disciplinary regulations. As the offence would not be punished until 10 days later, however, 'TC' was available to play.

Bristol Rovers: Sheppard, Roberts, Parsons, Green, Taylor, Prince, Stephens, W. Jones, Allan, Bannister, Godfrey. Substitute: B. Jones

Sheffield United: McAlister, Goulding, Hemsley, MacKenzie, Colquhoun, Hockey, Woodward, Salmons, Dearden, Currie, Scullion. Substitute: Eddy

Attendance: 19,768

The game began in a carnival atmosphere with bright summer weather. Flower beds adorned the areas behind the goals at Rovers' Eastville ground. The match ball was delivered by parachutists and Watney's ale was flowing in abundance – there were no restrictions on alcohol at grounds back then!

With the bit between their teeth and fired up by their victories over higher League opposition in the competition, Rovers set off at a high tempo, dominating a first half in which United appeared lethargic at best. All the invention and flair came from the home side, with Welsh international midfielder Wayne Jones prominent in their attacks. The solidity of United's defence was crucial in holding their opponents at bay, with Goulding, MacKenzie and Colquhoun all resolute in the tackle. Nevertheless, the Blades were thankful for the excellent form of young 'keeper Tom McAlister, the 19-year-old making three outstanding saves in an eight-minute period to keep the game tied. First, 'Tommo' dived across goal to keep out Brian Godfrey's powerful free-kick, and seconds later he flung himself to the right to claw away Bruce Bannister's header. Bannister was again denied as Tommo dived full length, stretching to turn a shot away from the top corner.

United re-emerged after the interval to play more like themselves. In particular, Tony Currie now began to impose himself in midfield as Rovers began to tire and space began to open up. Prompted by Currie's excellent passing, opportunities began to open up for the Blades. The service from the flanks was poor, however, and when good chances did present themselves to Scullion and Hockey neither man could hit the target. Unlike McAlister, who had kept United in the game, Rovers 'keeper Dick Sheppard's work was confined mainly to picking off a succession of hopeful crosses played into the penalty area. It could not be argued that the Blades were not trying hard, however, as the game was being played like a Cup tie, and the commitment from both sets of players saw three men booked: Trevor Hockey for United; Ken Stephens and Sandy Allen for Bristol Rovers.

With the game goalless after 90 minutes, the decision went down to penalties as extra-time was not being played. Rovers went first, and after the first compulsory five kicks no one had missed – Woodward, Eddie, Currie, Dearden and Colquhoun all scoring for United – and so it was time for sudden death. Rovers made it 6–5, Scullion equalised and the Pirates again scored to lead 7–6. It now came round to Ted Hemsley, a player who had previously taken, and scored, penalties for the Blades, most notably when saving a last-minute point at Loftus Road in the 1970–71 promotion season. Facing Dick Sheppard, Hemsley tried to place the ball to the 'keeper's left, only to see Shepherd gratefully smother the weakly-hit shot. The Blades, therefore, lost their first-ever penalty shoot-out. While Shepherd was delighted, Ted Hemsley, the unfortunate man to miss, was later critical of his effort, saying 'I always hit them, never tap them with the inside of the foot. But when I went up, I was so scared of missing that I decided to play safe place. The goalkeeper guessed right and that was that.'

Victory meant everything to Bristol Rovers. The management could even afford to accept Sheppard throwing his shirt to the crowd in celebration. The cost of such an act would have been prohibitive a year ago, according to their managing director Bill Dodgin, but on this great day in Rovers' history, such behaviour was allowed. With the Rovers players celebrating and parading the Cup, United's players were left in receipt of their runners'-up tankards, ironically made in Sheffield. It had been a week of travelling for the Blades players and fans, and it had ultimately ended in disappointment. Manager John Harris, ever the gentleman, congratulated the victorious Rovers side, although he also indicated that his own side's attacking performance had not been good enough. Hopefully, however, the competition had given United the rigorous workout they needed and they would hit the ground running in their second season back in the top flight.

Birmingham City 1–2 Sheffield United Division One

12 August 1972

Newly promoted to the top flight, the Blues had a decent team, and in particular a very strong forward line. The most prominent member of Birmingham's strike force was teenage marvel Trevor Francis, who was later to play for England and become the Football League's first £1 million player when signed by Brian Clough for Nottingham Forest. Almost equally impressive was Birmingham's centre-forward, Bob Latchford. He would later move on to Everton and, like Francis, also play for England. Also up front for the Blues was Bob Hatton, who would later play for the Blades in Division Four, in the process creating a great strike partnership with Keith Edwards. The Blues would prove a difficult proposition at St Andrew's, given that they had the longest unbeaten home record in all four divisions of the Football League. Ironically, although their run had continued for 36 games, they had last been defeated at home by United, who won 1–0 on 10 October 1970 in United's promotion-winning season.

With the successful introduction of young players into the United first team at the end of the 1971–72 season, in particular Tom McAlister in goal and Ian MacKenzie at centre-half, the Blades were hopeful of a good start to the new campaign. The signing of Keith Eddy for £50,000 from Watford was also designed to strengthen United's defensive and midfield capabilities. The Blades were, therefore, entering the season with some optimism, but also with a touch of realism. As the *Star's* Peter Howard noted in his assessment of

United's chances at the start of the season, 'United know just how good their players can be at their best. The problem is one of trying to maintain the highest level of all-round consistency throughout the season.' In the United boardroom there was a great sense of optimism, underlined by the announcement on Monday 7 August that the club would be carrying out £1.25 million worth of ground improvements, with priority given to the building of a 'fourth side' seating stand with a capacity of 8,000, which would be started in August 1973 and completed within a year at a cost of at least £650,000. In reality, the new South Stand's costs were to spiral upwards and it also was not actually opened until later – in August 1975. Interestingly, the new Bramall Lane stand, opened in 1966, had cost just £100,000.

United chairman Dick Wragg was optimistic for the future. He told the *Star* that the club would be able to handle the heavy investment they had become committed to, 'The directors have the utmost confidence in Sheffield United, otherwise we wouldn't have embarked on a project of this size.' At a shareholders meeting on 10 October, Wragg reiterated the reasons why the board had sanctioned the huge spending: it was to raise gate receipts through an increased numbers of seats, which would ultimately mean that 'Sheffield United will go to the very top'. Only such increased revenues could guarantee that the Blades could compete at the top end of the market for players, wages and transfer fees.

At St Andrew's the Blades were going to have to do without star man Tony Currie. 'TC' had decided not to appeal against his sending-off against Peterborough in the Watney Cup, meaning an absence of three games. In addition, Len Badger was still injured, and so for the first time for eight seasons, Len would miss the season's opener. With United forced into changes, Curry was replaced by Keith Eddy, making his League debut, and Badger by Steve Goulding. Manager John Harris, expecting a tough game, remarked, 'It is a pity we have to start this time with injury worries, which we didn't have a year ago, and this is a tough one to start with.' Birmingham, however, would be unchanged from the side that had beaten Stoke 4–3 on penalties in the FA Cup third-place match, which had been played the previous Saturday. Thanks to the traditional draw of the first game of the season and the Blues' return to the top flight, an excellent crowd of almost 38,000 were present at St Andrew's for the kick-off.

Birmingham City: Cooper, Carroll, Want, Campbell, Hynd, Harland, Hope, Francis, Latchford, Taylor. Substitute: Pendrey
Sheffield United: McAlister, Goulding, Hemsley, MacKenzie, Colquhoun, Hockey, Woodward, Salmons, Dearden, Eddy, Scullion. Substitute: Reece, replacing MacKenzie
Referee: Mr A. Oliver
Attendance: 37,390

Birmingham emerged to a rapturous reception from their fans, and the game set off at a pulsating rate as both sides pushed for an early goal. The determination of Blues fans to see their team off to a winning start was shown early by the booing that greeted Trevor Hockey's first touch of the ball. Ex-Birmingham captain Hockey had been a fans' favourite at St Andrew's prior to his transfer to the Blades in January 1971, but similar treatment followed him to the end of the game.

In the first couple of minutes teenager Trevor Francis stretched his boot high into the air, catching United's central-defender Ian MacKenzie in the face. The striker escaped a booking, but MacKenzie required treatment to a nasty cut, which, though taped, continued to bleed throughout the first half as the gutsy Bladesman stuck to his defensive duties. After just six minutes bad luck struck again as Eddie Colquhoun tried to knock Francis's through ball across to MacKenzie, only for the ball to bounce off the latter's shins and rebound into the path of the marauding Bob Latchford, who steered it wide of an exposed Tom McAlister's right hand and into the back of the net to put the home side a goal up.

With the St Andrew's crowd exploding into noise to celebrate the opening goal, the old adage of football struck yet again: a team is at its most vulnerable just after it has scored. Within a minute United had worked the ball to the edge of their opponent's penalty area and Trevor Hockey caught Paul Cooper slightly off his line and fired in a 25-yard shot that went over the City 'keeper's despairing dive and then dipped just under the bar to make it 1–1. As Hockey was subjected to another round of abuse, the tough midfielder humorously faced his tormenters to conduct, with his hands, the 'choir' of Birmingham browbeaters.

After such a frenetic start, the game settled down as both defences established a degree of composure. Yet there was certainly no lack of effort and, given that City were a tough, physical side, the Blades had to be strong to compete. After 17 minutes referee Mr Oliver believed that Eddie Colquhoun had been a little too robust and cautioned the Blades captain for what he perceived to be obstruction against Francis. Shortly after, Ian MacKenzie, already cut and injured, collided with United right-back Steve Goulding. Following further treatment, MacKenzie was left limping and, after temporarily being moved out to the right, was substituted after 20 minutes. With forward Gil Reece on the bench unable to come on as a like-for-like replacement, United were forced to reshuffle the side, with new man Keith Eddy's versatility paying immediate dividends as he was slotted in at centre-half besides Eddie Colquhoun, while MacKenzie was pushed up front to see if he could recover.

As the first half developed, Stewart Scullion was starting to create all types of problems for City's defence. Derek Allsopp noted in the *Telegraph* that Scullion almost single-handedly got the Blades through this critical period of the game when circumstances seemed to be conspiring against them, 'United's inspiration was Stewart Scullion. When the MacKenzie blow might have swung the match Birmingham's way, Scullion punctured so many holes in the home defence that all chance of gaining the initiative was lost.'

Scullion rattled the crossbar with a vicious, swerving 25-yard shot that had Cooper beaten, although the City 'keeper then brilliantly saved from Hockey's back header – United's midfielder relishing the hostile atmosphere and determined to silence his critics. Just before half-time and well on top, the Blades almost took the lead again when Scullion, scampering down the left wing, beat three defenders, cut inside and fired in a great shot that Cooper brilliantly tipped over the bar.

Unable to continue, MacKenzie was withdrawn at half-time to be replaced by Gil Reece. The physical nature of the contest was also underlined by Scullion's re-emergence with a bandaged right hand. United continued to look accomplished when in possession of the ball and went close early in the second half when Keith Eddy knocked a free-kick to Woodward, who drove the ball just wide of the post. Birmingham also applied pressure, with McAlister coming out to pick up a dangerous cross from Carroll with Hatton waiting to pounce. But after 58 minutes it was United who took the lead. Hockey, out on the left, worked enough room to cross the ball to Dearden. Centre-half Roger Hynd challenged United's centre-forward, only for the ball to break loose to the onrushing Alan Woodward, who proceeded to smash the ball past Cooper and into the corner of the net.

Stunned, Birmingham fought hard to get level, and the Blades suffered another injury as young McAlister bravely dived at the feet of Bob Latchford, smothering his goal-bound shot, but was left writhing on the ground in agony. Rallying around their shaken 'keeper, United's defence remained solid, allowing 'Tommo' to recover and go on to make another match-saving stop when he brilliantly turned Francis's overhead shot over the bar. As the game entered its final stages, Birmingham threw caution to the wind. The Blades, however, were resolute: a fantastic tackle from Keith Eddy denied Hynd and it was representative of their total commitment. With the full-time whistle blown, the Blades had got off to winning start in very difficult circumstances. Taunted by the Blues fans for the full 90 minutes, it was Trevor Hockey – along with his United teammates – who had the last laugh.

United's success without Currie at St Andrew's was not followed up in their next two games, however, both of which were at the Lane. The Blades were defeated by both Leeds and Newcastle, and the inspiration of United's talismanic midfielder was clearly seen as, on his return, their form picked up and they were beaten just once in their next six League games. This was a pleasing run of form given the injuries to key players, such as Keith Eddy, Stewart Scullion, Ian MacKenzie, Geoff Salmons and Billy Dearden. Pleasing for the directors, the fans and the management was how well the succession of youngsters called upon to plug the gaps had performed: Steve Goulding for Len Badger, Steve Cammack for Billy Dearden and David Staniforth for Gil Reece and Alan Woodward.

With hope that the injury situation would slowly improve, the Blades seemed to be in a healthy position, well within striking distance of the European places following their victory over Arsenal at Bramall Lane on 7 October. There was every reason for optimism at this point in the season at Bramall Lane.

Sheffield United 3–0 West Bromwich Albion Division One

6 January 1973

T he grounds for optimism that had existed in early October had truly dissipated as United entered the new year and prepared to face West Bromwich Albion in a real relegation 'four pointer' on 6 January 1973. A horrific run of form saw the Blades win just once in the League, 2–1 at home to Leicester on 16 December, draw twice and lose nine times. The side had seemingly been reinforced with the arrival of Alan Warboys from Cardiff City in the latter part of September, with David Powell and Gil Reece going in the opposite direction. Warboys, however, was to make just seven League appearances in the whole of the season without scoring, and his signing could be considered an unmitigated disaster. The longer-term injuries to Scullion, Salmons and Eddy during this period really began to hit home. United's younger players, except 'keeper Tom McAlister, who was continuing to produce excellent performances, were unable to maintain their form and were thus unable to hold down a place in the team in the long term. Just like in the 1971–72 season, there were not enough experienced players to successfully bring into the line up in the case of loss of form or injury.

Having lost three games in a row prior to West Brom's visit – 2–0 at Tottenham, followed by a 3–0 defeat to the eventual champions Liverpool at Bramall Lane on Boxing Day and a stiff 4–1 defeat by Newcastle – the vultures were circling and the knives were being sharpened up at the Lane. In reality, the performances had not been disastrous, but with football a results business, both supporters and members of the local media were distinctly unhappy as they saw a Division One table that, after 24 games, had United on 19 points, just two ahead of rock-bottom Manchester United. The only ray of hope for the Blades was that a cluster of clubs were struggling at the bottom: four on 19 points like United – including West Brom – and the bottom 12 clubs covered by just seven points.

The Blades were thrown into further disarray just the day before the game when Stewart Scullion put in a transfer request, following the announcement from John Harris that young Mick Speight, who had replaced the sick winger and played well at Newcastle, would retain his place, with Scullion on the bench. Wrist and cartilage injuries had seriously restricted Scullion's appearances following a superb opening season with the Blades and, clearly, the winger was frustrated with life at the Lane. Manager John Harris was far from impressed with the timing of the request, declaring, 'I am disappointed Stewart reacted in this way. It is the last thing we want at a time like this.' Meanwhile, in an attempt to strengthen the United squad, Harris was reported to have been out on several spying missions in the search of fresh talent.

Harris, recognising the importance of the West Brom game and insistent that the Blades would be giving their all to win, issued a note of caution, 'It will be anything but easy. West Brom have several very good players in their side.' Harris's comment was indeed true. Albion had, in the previous month, paid £135,000 for Willie Johnston, the Scottish international winger from Rangers, and Leeds had just pulled out of the £170,000 deal for Albion's Scottish international midfielder Asa Hartford – the famous 'hole in the heart' affair. Len Cantello, John Wile, Alistair Robertson, Tony Brown and Alistair Brown were other quality players in the Throstles side and, under manager Don Howe, it was perhaps a surprise that they had struggled that season. With the Blades having beaten West Brom 2–1 at the Hawthorns back on 26 August, the more optimistic Blades fans were hopeful that their team could record their first League double of the season.

Sheffield United: McAlister, Badger, Hemsley, Flynn, MacKenzie, Eddy, Woodward, Salmons, Dearden, Currie, Speight. Substitute: Scullion, replacing Speight
West Bromwich Albion: Latchford, Nisbet, Robertson, Cantello, Wile, Merrick, Glover, T. Brown, A. Brown, Hartford, Johnston. Substitute: Woolgar
Referee: Mr J. Wrennall
Attendance: 16,231

It was a disappointing attendance, almost 18,000 down on the last home game against Liverpool. It reflected the pessimism surrounding Bramall Lane, and it was United's lowest attendance since returning to the First Division. With John Harris away on another spying mission, assistant John Short was in charge for the afternoon. Eddie Colquhoun, suffering from the flu, was replaced by Ian MacKenzie, while Ted Hemsley was making his 150th League appearance. In the absence of Colquhoun, Tony Currie was made captain for the day.

The visitors threatened from the start. In the very first minute the Blades had to be thankful for 'keeper Tom McAlister, who pulled off a fine save as he kept out Johnston's close-range header from Ally Brown's cross. Yet that near miss did not reflect the developing balance of play, as it was the Blades, throwing off any nerves, who went on to provide the Lane crowd with an impressive game of football, demonstrative of fine attacking play. Mick Speight, providing vigor and purpose on the left, played a great ball through to Alan Woodward, only for the winger to be fractionally offside. Wile and Robertson then combined to deny the ever-present threat of Billy Dearden. United's centre-forward then set off on a brilliant run down the right, reaching the goalline and pulling the ball back to the onrushing Currie, whose fizzing first-time shot was blocked by Robertson. With the Blades in firm control of midfield, the chances continued to come. An excellent move involving Salmons, Currie and Hemsley ended in a fine save by Latchford at his near post. It was all United, the visitors finding it hard to get any semblance of pattern or rhythm to their play, which 'fluctuated between the mediocre and pathetic' according to the *Sheffield Telegraph*'s Derek Allsop.

After 17 minutes United's pressure finally told as they worked an excellent opening goal. Mick Speight, just inside the Albion half, played a defence-splitting pass to Currie, who pushed the ball into the path of Billy Dearden, who took the ball in his stride and hit a ferocious rising shot into the top of Latchford's net.

An injury to Speight, hurt by a late tackle, led to the young midfielder leaving the pitch for treatment, and the Blades were down to 10 men for the next few minutes. The one-man advantage briefly offered West Brom a way to get back into the game, but Speight's return, although he was clearly struggling, again provided more opportunity for the increasingly-influential Currie to pull the strings in midfield. It was no surprise, therefore, that the Blades continued to create chances, and in the 43rd minute they had their second goal, thanks to Dearden. Ted Hemsley, forcing his way down United's left, crossed into the area and Dearden, hovering on the edge of the six-yard line, rose to head past Latchford.

Troubled by his injury, Mick Speight did not return after half-time and was replaced by Stewart Scullion. The Albion team had clearly suffered a half-time dressing down and initially emerged with more determination. Hartford produced a fine shot that was just wide and, for a short time, United's defence was finally being forced to work hard to protect their lead. Yet they were soon back to providing business as usual as Albion's new-found resolve faded and the Blades, through the twin threats of Currie and Dearden in particular, began to re-impose themselves on the game. The signal for United's return to control was a brilliant through ball by Tony Currie after 50 minutes to the elusive Dearden, who, beating the offside trap and running almost half the length of the field, was only denied his hat-trick goal by a brilliant save from Albion 'keeper Peter Latchford. Soon afterwards another great move, initiated by 'TC', ended with Dearden rounding Latchford, only for Gordon Nisbet to scramble away Billy's goal-bound shot. From the resultant corner, after 52 minutes, Woodward delivered a precise in-swinging ball to the near post, where Ian MacKenzie rose to head past Latchford to make it 3–0.

The Blades were playing magnificently, the nerves had gone and the crowd were revelling in this long-awaited performance. MacKenzie's goal had effectively killed the game; there was no way back for Albion and the only surprise was how United, continuing to pour forward, failed to add to their lead. Currie weaved past two men and shot just wide of the far post, United won a succession of corners, one of which was hacked off the line by Robertson, and Latchford produced a great save, diving full length to keep out John Flynn's header.

Triumphant, the Blades had lifted the gloom at Bramall Lane – at least for a week! Assistant manager John Short, in his after-match assessment, declared, 'This is more like it. Our game started flowing much better today. We are quite satisfied.' So were the local media, Peter Howard noting in the *Green 'Un* that 'it was cheers instead of jeers at Bramall Lane this afternoon and it is hard to see United suffering relegation when they can turn in a performance like this.' Singled out for special praise were Tony Currie and Billy Dearden. Derek Allsop noted in Currie's performance a growing maturity that could take him on to become a top international player, 'There was involvement and application not always seen in his game, qualities which have threatened to stand between him and greatness, and he garnished it all with half a dozen succulent first-time flicks into the path of his raiding colleagues.' The praise was just as effusive for the United centre-forward, 'Bill Dearden is a man you just cannot keep down. He is essentially a team man, the kind of player who runs his heart and soul out for 90 minutes and doesn't always see his efforts rewarded.'

Dearden's two goals had provided confidence for the team and had brought his total goals for the season to 10. Billy was to go on to grab 20 League goals that season, the last Blades player to score that many in the top flight. With strong performances also from Flynn and Speight in the first half, there was a genuine hope that the Blades had turned the corner.

Yet Harris's absence was a clear indication that he felt that the team needed to be strengthened, particularly in the goal-scoring department. Unfortunately though, new additions were not forthcoming in the next few weeks. The Albion game saw a mini-run of four undefeated matches for the Blades. A very disappointing 2–1 defeat at Second Division Carlisle in the fourth round of the FA Cup on 3 February saw United enter a period in which they took just two points out of their next five League games. As a result, the battle for First Division survival was clearly still on.

Sheffield United 2–1 Manchester United Division One

23 April 1973

Still in trouble near the foot of the table in early March, United's fortunes were to take an upturn as their League form gradually improved and the team began to put in more consistent performances. Arguably, two key additions in personnel brought the improvement. Keith Eddy had been signed from Watford for £50,000 shortly before the start of the season. He had come on as a substitute to take a penalty in the pre-season Watney Cup Final at Bristol Rovers, and had started the first three League games, only to be sidelined by tendon trouble for a couple of months. Returning to play at Charlton in the League Cup in October, he aggravated his tendon further and only made it back to the first team in time for the 6 January game against West Brom. With John Harris keeping the midfielder in the team, Eddy's match fitness gradually improved and he was to have a growing and stabilising influence in the centre of midfield, a perfect foil for the flamboyance of Tony Currie.

Eddy's elevation to the side was at the expense of Trevor Hockey. Hockey was becoming unsettled at the club and put in a transfer request shortly after the West Brom game. Hockey's availability, given that the board and John Harris were prepared to sell him, eventually fitted in with Harris's desire to get a striker to provide additional support for Billy Dearden following the relative failure of Alan Warboys. Harris, in the latter part of February, was able to exchange Trevor Hockey and £30,000 with Norwich for their

Scottish international striker Jim Bone. At 23 years of age, Harris had brought Bone to Bramall Lane as a proven striker who was still young enough to be developed as a player. The young Scot was to prove a very good exchange for the 30-year-old Trevor Hockey in United's relegation battle.

Bone made his debut in the goalless draw at Leicester on 24 February and provided an immediate bonus for John Harris in that he immediately struck up a superb understanding with his new strike partner Billy Dearden. In 10 League games, prior to the meeting with Manchester United, Bone scored six times and Dearden five times. United's form had dramatically improved and much of it was down to this dynamic duo, 'They go together like Flanagan and Allan, or should I say Morecambe and Wise', noted John Harris in mid-April. Scoring crucial goals, Jim had quickly become a fans' favourite and the Blades were now clear of the relegation places and were looking forward to another season of First Division football when they visited Old Trafford.

Like the Blades, Manchester United had experienced a very difficult season. Bottom of the League at the turn of the year, the Reds had appointed Tommy Docherty as their new manager, and his growing influence meant that the team, like the Blades, had managed to improve markedly over the previous couple of months. The Reds had gone on an excellent run and had guaranteed their First Division survival at the time of United's visit.

Given that the game had all the appearances of an end-of-season fixture with nothing at stake, both teams could have been forgiven for taking a relaxed attitude towards proceedings. One factor, however, meant that this would not be just another game. This was the match that marked the great Bobby Charlton's farewell to Old Trafford. It was his final League appearance at the end of a season that would bring his retirement from playing. World Cup winner Bobby had played 106 times for England and was the country's record goalscorer with 49 international goals. He was also Manchester United's record appearance maker, having topped 600 League games during the course of the season. A 'Busby Babe', Charlton had survived the Munich Air Crash and had gone on to win the League title and the FA and European Cups with the Reds. It had been a glorious career full of achievement. Yet, as the great Matt Busby noted in the match programme, Bobby was not just a great footballing talent, but a real gentleman too, 'Here we have the model player…I hold him in the greatest respect as a man, an example not only at Old Trafford, but for the whole of Football. When things looked their blackest after the Munich accident, I was cheered enormously to think that Bobby Charlton was there. His presence was a great source of inspiration to keep working for the restoration of Manchester United. He has broken all records and won everything possible. Yet he has remained completely unspoiled.'

Manchester United: Stepney, Young, Sidebottom, Graham, Holton, Buchan, Morgan, Charlton, Macari, Martin.
Sheffield United: McAlister, Badger, Hemsley, MacKenzie, Faulkner, Eddy, Scullion, Salmons, Dearden, Currie, Bone.
Referee: Mr C. Thomas
Attendance: 55,035

With injuries to John Flynn and Eddie Colquhoun, United gave a debut to young centre-half Steve Faulkner. At just 18 years of age, Faulkner was playing on one of the biggest stages in English football. In the Manchester United side was Brian Kidd – later to be assistant manager to both Neil Warnock and Bryan Robson at Bramall Lane – and young teenager Arnold Sidebottom, who was being given his Manchester United debut by Tommy Docherty. Sidebottom would later become better known to Blades fans in his guise as an excellent bowler for Yorkshire – he would, in fact, prove a far more successful cricketer.

With Manchester United having survived relegation and the nostalgia surrounding Bobby Charlton, there was an atmosphere of euphoria at Old Trafford, with young fans invading the pitch chanting for Bobby before the game began. Even though the young fans were good-natured on such a special occasion, in an area of serious football hooliganism such behaviour was severely censured by the media. Andrew Tatham, writing in the *Sheffield Telegraph*, made comments typical of his colleagues in the press when describing the scene, 'The genuine villains of the peace were the hordes of unruly youngsters…the pitch exploded into a fusion of garish colours as the so-called supporters flocked towards the players' entrance.'

When Bobby Charlton and the teams emerged, Tony Currie, as acting Blades captain, presented the England star with an inscribed tray made of Sheffield plate, but as the game got underway it was clear that the Blades had no intention of taking it easy on the Mancunians. Straight from the kick-off it was the Blades who were the most impressive. With Tony Currie and Keith Eddy taking firm control of midfield, all the early creative play and chances came from the Blades. Yet it was the Reds who went into the lead after 13 minutes, as debutant Steve Faulkner under-hit a backpass to Tom McAlister and Brian Kidd gleefully ran on and planted the ball past the Sheffield 'keeper to make it 1–0 to the hosts, whose fans now believed that they were on their way to marking Bobby Charlton's curtain call with victory. The goal was a devastating moment for Steve Faulkner and the mistake could have seriously undermined the youngster's confidence. To his credit, however, Faulkner put the incident behind him and went on to produce a strong defensive display for the rest of the game.

Fortunately, the Blades were not behind for long. After 22 minutes Ted Hemsley chipped the ball over a static Manchester United defence who, pleading for an offside flag that was not going to come, had to watch as Billy Dearden raced through the middle after the ball. Reds 'keeper Alex Stepney was quick off his line and almost dived successfully to take the ball from the onrushing centre-forward. Billy, however, was first and took the ball from Stepney's grasp and shot it into the empty net to make it 1–1 and silence the Old Trafford crowd. From this point on it was all the Blades, with Keith Eddy really coming to the fore. Initially brought in to provide stability to the midfield, on the great stage of Old Trafford he was putting on a masterclass in inventive and imaginative midfield play, outshining even 'TC' himself. It was therefore fitting that it was Keith Eddy who scored the winner, crashing home an unstoppable 30-yard shot past Alex Stepney, an example of great technique and control.

Winning 2–1, Sheffield United's dominance had not been truly reflected in the scoreline. Manchester United's performance had been pedestrian and out of step with the cultured and skilful approach epitomised by Bobby Charlton, the man the crowd had come to honour. For the Blades it was a satisfying victory, and a high profile one too, given the national television news coverage of the game. An away draw against Ipswich on 28 April and a 3–2 home victory over Tottenham to end the season on 2 May, provided a satisfactory conclusion to what had been a very difficult season. The fans had now been given some hope that, barring the injury problems that had blighted the start of United's present campaign, next season would be better.

Unfortunately, Steve Faulkner never quite developed into the top-flight centre-half that the Blades were looking for, and he made just another 13 League appearances before moving on to York City at the end of the 1976–77 season. Nevertheless, having played in such a high-profile match, he certainly had some great memories to carry into his post-football life.

Sheffield United 5–0 Arsenal
Division One

4 September 1973

The improvement in form at the end of the 1972–73 campaign had given Blades fans some hope for the new season. John Harris made just one signing over the summer, utility man Colin Franks from Watford for £55,555. Franks, however, was not to play much of a role in his first season with the club. The opening game against newly-promoted Burnley at Bramall Lane on 25 August proved disappointing as the Blades went down 2–0, despite creating some good chances. The widening of the Lane pitch by a couple of yards, the issuing of personal overnight travelling bags to the players and officials, and a new-look strip were all unable to get the Blades off to a winning start. The club was particularly proud of the new kit, the match programme for the game against Arsenal hoping that 'supporters too, will be enthusiastic about seeing their favourites in modern, updated gear.' The strip sported collars on the shirts and continental-style numbers on the shorts. Clearly, the club believed that such innovations would lead to a happy dressing room as 'it is the small things which are appreciated by the players.'

After losing 2–0 at Wolverhampton Wanderers on the following Tuesday night, although having played well again, the Blades finally got their campaign under way with a pleasing 2–1 victory against Chelsea at Stamford Bridge, with goals courtesy of Tony Currie and Alan Woodward. This then brought United around to the eagerly-anticipated visit of Arsenal on Tuesday 4 September. Arsenal had continued to be a powerful side following their double success of 1970–71, and they had ended the previous season as

Great new poster of Tony...plus team pic

Hot from the presses! New poster of Tony Currie—10p . . . Glossy team picture, 5p, in the Lane Shop **TONIGHT!**

The new icon celebrated. 'TC' attains cult status at the Lane.

runners-up in both the League and FA Cup. The Gunners had also inflicted one of United's most humiliating defeats in recent memory when crushing the Blades 5–0 at Bramall Lane on 29 January 1972, with Alan Ball adding insult to injury by sitting on the football during play to emphasise his team's superiority. The Blades had lost two out of their three games against Arsenal the previous season, but this time, buoyed by the victory at Stamford

Bridge, manager John Harris expected his squad to be equal to the task. Previewing the game, the United boss declared, 'They are a top-class side, no question about it. They are a good team, difficult to beat and well organised. It's a great challenge and I'm sure our lads will take it up – it brings the best out of us.'

There were two interesting subplots to the game. The first involved the competing claims of United's Tony Currie and Arsenal's Alan Ball and Charlie George for a place in England's midfield. 'TC' had performed brilliantly in United's first three games, and with Ball suspended for England's game against Austria later in the month, Currie had to be uppermost in the mind of England boss Alf Ramsey. The second brought the opportunity to compare the relative merits of Bob Wilson and Tom McAlister for the Scottish goalkeeper's jersey. Wilson, the present incumbent, had the years of experience, while McAlister was a promising and upcoming young talent.

Sheffield United: McAlister, Badger, Hemsley, Flynn, Colquhoun, Eddy, Woodward, Salmons, Dearden, Currie, Bone.
Arsenal: Wilson, Rice, McNab, Batson, Blockley, Storey, Armstrong, Ball, Kelly, Kennedy, George.
Referee: Mr D. Turner
Attendance: 27,839

With large numbers of fans not turning up until after 7:15 for a 7:30 kick-off, thousands were unfortunately left waiting to get through the turnstiles as, from its first moments, the match exploded into life. It was the Blades who lit the touchpaper as, in the first 20 minutes, they produced, in the words of the *Star's* Tony Pritchett, 'the most damaging and destructive display of total football I have ever seen.'

In the first minute Tony Currie combined with Keith Eddy, who fed the ball out to Alan Woodward. The winger then played an inviting ball into the box and Billy Dearden, reacting much quicker than Arsenal centre-half Jeff Blockley, steered the ball past Wilson to make it 1–0 with just 35 seconds on the clock. On top, the Blades continued to pour forward, while the Arsenal defence, in particular expensive £200,000 signing Jeff Blockley, had a torrid time. After nine minutes Currie beat Arsenal's Peter Storey, only to be brought down on the edge of the area. Getting up quickly, 'TC' knocked the free-kick back to Alan Woodward, who smashed his right-footed shot along the ground and through the packed defence into the corner of Wilson's net. At 2–0 up, the Blades were rampant. Two minutes later Billy Dearden slipped a pass to Tony Currie who, from 30 yards, smashed a shot that simply flew past Wilson and into the top left-hand corner of the Arsenal net. Basking in the adulation of the fans, Currie blew his now-customary kisses to the crowd. With 17 minutes gone United had their fourth goal as Geoff Salmons launched a long throw to Jim

Bone, who advanced towards the goal and, unchecked by Blockley, proceeded to drill another long-range shot past the shell-shocked Wilson. Two minutes later it was almost five as Dearden raced on to a through ball, with the Arsenal defence in disarray, only for his resulting shot to cannon back off Wilson's left-hand post with the Arsenal 'keeper thoroughly beaten.

To their credit, Arsenal's heads did not drop and the feisty Alan Ball was working hard to get his side going. After 22 minutes it was Ball who robbed Currie and fired in a shot that smashed against McAlister's right-hand post. With United's opening barrage having effectively won the game, the intensity of the match inevitably dropped and play became more even. After 35 minutes it was Ball again who also almost reduced the deficit, diverting an Arsenal corner towards goal, only to see Ted Hemsley hook the ball off the line.

Yet for all Alan Ball's determination, the Blades continued to dominate proceedings. Currie was at his sharpest and swept aside the infamous Peter Storey, Arsenal's hardman in midfield, whose job was to stifle the opposition's creative talent. Keith Eddy was also showing just how well he had taken to top flight football. A calming influence in midfield, his creative passing and quick thinking was much in evidence. At the back, John Flynn and Eddie Colquhoun were assured in the centre, while Badger and Hemsley were foraging forward in support of the attack, where Woodward, Salmons, Bone and Dearden were pulling the Gunners defence to pieces. It was truly a great team performance.

Fifteen minutes into the second half the Blades had their fifth goal. It was a superbly-worked effort between Salmons and Currie, the former playing a brilliantly-weighted return pass to Currie, who thumped the ball wide of the diving Wilson. The question now was whether United's star midfielder could get his hat-trick goal as the team continued to create a host of chances. It was not to be, however, and although George Armstrong hit the bar for Arsenal late on, the Gunners could have no complaints about the scale of their defeat. All that was left was for Tony Currie to exact revenge for Alan Ball's humiliating stunt of two seasons ago. With time running out, Currie sat on the football during play, so underlining United's superiority. Sportingly, Currie recalled after the game, 'Alan Ball took it well, laughing all over his face.' It was a key moment for Currie, underlining his elevation to true iconic status among the fans who, for some time, had realised what a truly special talent he was. The following night *The Sheffield Star* had a picture of 'TC' sat on the football and relaxing with a cup of tea. The caption 'True You Can Do Magic' was a reference to the signature tune he was becoming associated with at the Lane: the number-one hit by Limmie and the Family Cooking in the summer of 1973, regularly played by club DJ Ian Ramsay.

Manager John Harris was obviously delighted with the result. It was a vindication of his players given that the manager had refused to be negative over their first two League defeats of the season. Harris had maintained that the players were performing well, creating chances and working together. The success against Arsenal, coming on the back of the Stamford Bridge victory, proved to Harris that 'we've got a good team here… [they were] simply magnificent, every one of them did Sheffield proud.'

The win did not, unfortunately, act as a catalyst for United to move to the next level, which could have seen them challenge for honours. The Blades proved to be inconsistent: excellent at times, average at others. During the remainder of September the team won two, lost two and drew one of their five League games, establishing themselves firmly as a mid-table side: too good to be embroiled in a relegation battle, but with little hope of reaching the higher echelons of the League table.

Match 15

Sheffield United 4–2 Southampton Division One

22 December 1973

United's form prior to the Southampton game was not helped by injuries and the loss of form of key players. Goalkeeper Tom McAlister's broken leg in the game against Manchester City at Bramall Lane on 20 October was a cruel blow for the youngster, still just 20 years of age, and his replacement proved a real problem. Manager John Harris had to choose between reserves John Connaughton, signed from Manchester United for £20,000, and John Hope, United's regular 'keeper in the 1971–72 season, and more recently on loan at Preston. Harris initially chose Connaughton, but he was clearly not of the same calibre as McAlister. This period also saw the absence of Keith Eddy, who was out for almost three months after he broke his collarbone at Norwich on 22 September. Fortunately for the Blades, Eddy returned as a substitute against Everton on 15 December and would be back in the starting line up for the Southampton match.

Just as worrying for the Blades was the lack of productivity from their strike force; the Jim Bone/Billy Dearden partnership, which had destroyed opposition defences at the latter end of the 1972–73 season and at the beginning of the next, was no longer firing on all cylinders. Dearden, who had bagged 20 League goals in the previous campaign, had just two to his name in 18 League appearances, while Bone had not scored since the away fixture at Tottenham on 15 September.

Nevertheless, the team were holding on to a mid-table position, and in their last home game against Derby on 17 November (the weather postponing an early December fixture against Ipswich) the Blades had won convincingly 3–0 and were widely applauded for their exciting attacking football in beating an incredibly talented Rams side.

New United boss Ken Furphy.

The winds of change were blowing at Bramall Lane, however, and on 6 December the Blades officially unveiled their new manager, Ken Furphy of Blackburn Rovers. The United board had decided that for the team to move forward, they needed a younger manager who was more in tune with the modern demands of the game. John Harris would be retained, as he had been when United's board had moved to replace him with Arthur Rowley prior to the 1968–69 season. Harris's role, though, was ill-defined. Chairman Dick Wragg – having reminded United's fans and the media that his relationship with Harris had been the 'longest chairman-manager partnership in football' – noted that Mr Harris would be 'minister without portfolio'. John Harris's real commitment to the club he clearly loved was shown in his own comment that 'Anything I can do for Sheffield United will do for me.' Nevertheless, although replaced, it seemed that Harris had approved of United's appointment of Furphy, who had made a good reputation in the game through his work at Watford and Blackburn. Certainly, Harris had signed several of Furphy's Watford players, including Currie, Scullion, Eddy and Franks.

Taking over the team officially on Friday 7 December, Furphy joined up with the players on the coach as they travelled down to London to face Queen's Park Rangers. The team had already been chosen by Harris, and against a good Rangers side they achieved a very creditable goalless draw. Returning to United, Furphy announced that he would take the first-team squad to Lilleshall on Monday for four days so that he could get to know the squad better. One player who he knew lots about was Tony Currie, who, Furphy indicated, had forced him to hang up his boots as player-manager at Watford. The young, precocious talent had taken his manager's position in the Watford side. After Lilleshall, the Blades visited Everton on 15 December, again playing well and securing a draw: 1–1, courtesy of an Eddie Colquhoun goal.

Furphy's more modern media-savvy approach, in comparison to the more restrained nature of Harris, was nowhere more evident to Blades fans than when they opened up the matchday programme for the Southampton game. Ken Furphy announced his arrival with the inaugural manager's column. Whereas other clubs had, for quite some time, moved towards giving managers a direct outlet for their views to the fans through the club programme, United and John Harris had not seen this form of communication as important. More significantly, Furphy used his first article as a rallying point for the fans. He was particularly keen to show them that there were no limits to his ambitions for the club and to his expectations. Boldly, the new boss declared, 'My aim: to be recognised as a "super-club"'. Furphy commended the warmth of the staff and the 'willingness to make my new task as easy as possible', but, he made clear, 'I also intend to instil a fierce desire throughout the club to be successful'.

On the pitch, Furphy acknowledged that Harris had produced a good team, impressive at QPR, and it was 'a case of adding extra dimensions to the team's play so that we can go forward'.

Interestingly, visitors Southampton had only recently confirmed their own new team manager's appointment. Lawrie McMenemy had held the position of 'manager designate' since the start of the campaign, following his successful period in charge of Grimsby Town. Long-standing Saints manager Ted Bates had now finally moved upstairs to become the club's chief executive. Southampton were doing particularly well, and lay fifth in the table, five points clear of United, who would clearly face a tough task on Ken Furphy's first appearance before the Bramall Lane faithful.

Sheffield United: Connaughton, Badger, Hemsley, Flynn, Colquhoun, Speight, Woodward, Eddy, Staniforth, Currie, Salmons. Substitute: Bone
Southampton: Martin, McCarthy, Mills, Fisher, Bennett, Steele, Paine, Channon, Gilchrist, Byrne, Stokes. Substitute: O'Brien
Referee: Mr R. Tinkler
Attendance: 17,173

Furphy, dressed in a tracksuit, chose to lead out the Blades side and was given a warm welcome by the Bramall Lane crowd. They were without Billy Dearden, replaced by David Staniforth, but Keith Eddy was brought back into the starting line up following his successful reintroduction to the side as a substitute in the previous game at Everton.

As if they were keen to impress under the new regime, the Blades started at breakneck speed, forcing two corners in the opening exchanges. Alan Woodward's fierce goal-bound drive was charged down in the box, and Salmons, bursting through the Saints defence, shot narrowly wide. Southampton had their moments too, particularly when Channon headed a free-kick straight down into the path of Fisher, who blazed the ball high over the bar with a clear sight of goal. The high tempo continued, as a clever interchange of passes between Tony Currie and Billy Dearden released Geoff Salmons down the left, whose teasing centre was scrambled away by the Saints defence. But after 17 minutes it was the visitors who almost took the lead, as Channon expertly bent a free-kick around the Blades' wall on the edge of the area, only for Connaughton to produce a good diving save. Three minutes later the Blades were

Despite the close attention of the Saints' defence, 'Woody' puts United a goal up.

fortunate to remain level, as Saints full-back Steve Mills charged down the left flank and delivered a perfect pass into Paul Gilchrist, only for the striker to miskick the ball from just six yards out with the goal at his mercy.

Given the cracking start that United had experienced, this period of Southampton dominance was concerning the Lane faithful. Fortunately, however, it was a reminder to the Blades to get back on track, and Eddy and Currie combined to play in Alan Woodward, his fierce shot kept out by 'keeper Eric Martin's legs. After 27 minutes United's winger did finally get the ball in the opposition net and it came at the end of a superb attacking move. Geoff Salmons, out on the left, played in a beautiful long ball to Currie in the area. 'TC', aware of the players around him, knocked the ball down for Alan Woodward who, despite the close attentions of full-back Bob McCartney, was able to smash the ball low and hard into the corner of the net. Continuing to attack and threaten Martin's goal, the Blades had their second after 35 minutes. Keith Eddy started the move, playing the ball to Mick Speight, who moved it on to Currie, who found Salmons. Out on the left, Geoff Salmons played in another accurate cross, which Alan Woodward, unmarked in the area, dived full length to head the ball past Martin. A great goal, it was a rarity in the Woodward scoring archive, given that he rarely scored with headers.

The Blades seemed to have put themselves firmly in charge of the contest with Woodward's double strike, yet within just a minute the celebrations of the Lane crowd were muted as Paine and Stokes combined for the latter to cross into the area, where Paul Gilchrist ghosted in to glance a header past Connaughton and into United's net. Playing with renewed vigour, the Saints pressed forward, and in the final minute of the first half they drew level. Keith Eddy, unaware of Mick Channon's presence, played a backpass to Connaughton, only for Southampton's England striker to race in and smash the ball into the net to make it 2–2 at half-time. It was a desperate blow for the Blades, who, after 35 minutes, were seemingly well on the road to victory. Yet, to be fair, Southampton had played well in the first half and perhaps deserved some reward. Crucially for the Blades, they would now have to start all over again.

United emerged in a determined fashion after the break, with no evidence that their morale and purpose had been dented by the Saints' comeback. Almost immediately, Woodward and Currie linked cleverly, the former smashing in a powerful shot that was palmed away by Martin. The Southampton 'keeper had to be alert to the resultant corner, holding on well to Eddy Colquhoun's powerful header. The visitors were also attacking at every opportunity, the game opening up into a feast of attacking football as both sides went for the win. Connaughton saved well from Gilchrist's header, and then Stokes headed away a good effort by John Flynn from a Woodward corner.

After 58 minutes the Blades got back in front. Badger harried Steve Mills on the Saints goalline, forcing the left-back to concede a corner. Then came a moment of genius as Currie took the kick, pulling it back to Alan Woodward, who had taken a position five yards outside the penalty area. In a prearranged move, 'Woody', unmarked, smashed the ball as it dropped to him and his volley flew into the net for 3–2: a brilliant hat-trick goal.

Six minutes later the Blades struck again. A brilliant long ball by Keith Eddy found Woodward in the clear, and, as he advanced on goal, he looked about to notch his fourth strike of the game. Centre-half Paul Bennett managed to get back, however, and partially blocked the shot, but Tony Currie, up in support, picked up the rebound and drilled it past Martin and just inside the left-hand post to make it 4–2. Southampton tried hard to claw their way back into the game as Connaughton was soon forced into good saves from Gilchrist and Fisher. The Blades continued to be a danger, and, focused and resolute, United's defence were determined not to let their lead slip away again. When the referee brought proceedings to a close, the Blades had won by four goals to two.

It had been a superb game, full of fine football from both sides, 'a match to savour and to remember' according to the *Green 'Un's* Tony Pritchett. It was certainly a good game for new boss Ken Furphy to present himself to the Lane faithful. Just as in previous seasons, however, the spectre of inconsistency remained, and the Blades were a mid-table team who were unable to threaten the top positions. Injuries did not help the situation, either. Billy Dearden made no further appearances following the game at home to Spurs on 12 January and Billy's replacement, Terry Nicholl, scored just one goal in 10 appearances. Tony Currie missed five games in February and then the last seven matches of the season and John Flynn missed six games during March and April. One shining light, however, was Ken Furphy's signing of Jim Brown from Chesterfield in goal in March, the new boss realising that Connaughton and, latterly, the returning John Hope, were not up to the task of replacing Tom McAlister.

Match 16

Sheffield United 3–1 Ipswich Town Division One

31 August 1974

At the start of Ken Furphy's first full season in charge, the Blades had made a sound start. They had drawn against Queen's Park Rangers 1–1 on the opening day of the season at Bramall Lane, with Steve Cammack scoring, then had drawn 2–2 at Newcastle, with Eddy and Speight scoring. There then followed a 2–0 defeat at Derby, followed by a 2–1 home victory over Newcastle, with Steve Cammack and Tony Field scoring. This promising form was somewhat of a surprise to Blades fans, who had feared the worst following new chairman John Hassall's reiteration of the message that servicing the debt for the new South Stand was the club's priority and that success on the field, although important, would have to be pursued through real financial constraints. Ominously, Hassall's message seemed to stick in the minds of the fans, and attendances for the first two home fixtures (16,032 and 17,650 respectively) were extremely worrying for the board.

In the matchday programme for the Ipswich game, Ken Furphy declared, 'Our form so far has been encouraging, and facing Ipswich this afternoon it will be put to the test well and truly. Ipswich are a formidable outfit.' Ipswich had finished fourth in the previous two seasons and had qualified for Europe. This season they had made a tremendous start by gaining four successive wins. Arsenal had been beaten home and away, along with Burnley and Tottenham, and they had not conceded a goal. With a 100 per cent record, Ipswich were early leaders of the First Division. Furphy saw Ipswich as a template for United's own

if every
United fan...

found just a dozen or so friends who would like the
opportunity of winning hundreds of pounds for a
nominal 5p per week . . . the Blades would have
the largest fund-raising organisation in the country!

Come on, United fans—let's make this our target,
and become a United Development Agent NOW!

Our Agents receive plenty of special benefits,
because everyone at the Lane realises just how vital
their efforts are to the long-term success of the club.

★ ACT NOW! PLEASE DON'T LEAVE IT TO
SOMEONE ELSE. CALL OR WRITE FOR DETAILS
TO TERRY OSMOND. TELEPHONE 27901.

I wish to become an agent for Sheffield United
Football Club Development Fund.

Name

Address

Return to: Sheffield United Football Club,
Pools Office, Shoreham Street,
Sheffield.

An appeal for agents to help raise money
towards financing the proposed 'fourth
side' at Bramall Lane.

development, 'having done the ground work well, they are now benefiting from it'. That ground work, laid down by manager Bobby Robson, involved developing a fluent passing style of play, with many pundits declaring that they were the best footballing side in the country. A productive youth system meant a production line of excellent players, such as goalkeeper Laurie Sivell, right-back George Burley, midfielders Brian Talbot and Kevin Beattie, and forwards Trevor Whymark and Clive Woods. In addition, Robson had an ability to identify affordable talent from elsewhere, such as centre-half Allan Hunter from Blackburn and Bryan Hamilton from Linfield. Importantly, Ipswich were not a big club, in that they were able to top the table on average gates of under 25,000. This gave hope to others – especially United with their financial burdens – that it was possible to be competitive without having the resources of Liverpool, Leeds or Arsenal.

Regardless of his admiration for Bobby Robson's side, Furphy was confident that the Blades could win the game. In his pre-match interviews he reminded everyone that 'we were the last team to beat them when we had nothing like a full-strength side', a reference to United's one-goal victory on the final day of the previous season at Portman Road on 27 April. United were, however, entering the game with some disappointing news concerning young goalkeeper Tom McAlister. Having recovered from his broken leg, received against Manchester City back in October 1973, Tom had come back for pre-season training, only to sustain a hairline fracture over the original break in a friendly against Altrincham. A small plaster had been placed on the injury, but following its removal Tom suffered pain after jogging and doctors ordered a full-length cast to be placed on to the leg, effectively meaning that Tom would be out for a considerable period. Thankfully, Jim Brown had continued to prove an excellent buy and was giving management and fans few concerns over his performances.

Billy Dearden was another player who had experienced a long time on the sidelines through injury, but he was in a better situation than McAlister. Billy had been brought back into the starting line up against Ipswich due to Steve Cammack's inability to throw off an ankle injury sustained in the previous Tuesday night's game against Newcastle. Dearden had not started a game since 12 January against Tottenham at the Lane. Billy, with a history of serious cartilage trouble, had undergone an operation to remove a third cartilage after that game and now, after participation in the pre-season programme, was getting his opportunity. At 30 years of age, Dearden was at a difficult stage of his career and was desperate to make an impression. Interviewed before the game, he admitted to feeling nervous, given his long period away from the first team. The lack of depth to United's squad was illustrated by the fact that, in order to name a substitute for the game, Furphy drafted in young 19-year-old striker Gary France, who had made just one League appearance for the club.

Ipswich, meanwhile, were at full strength. David Johnson, the only injury concern following the midweek 3–0 win over Arsenal, was declared fit to play. With Ipswich strikers Trevor Whymark and Johnson in good form and particularly strong in the air, and midfielder Mick Lambert having scored three times in four games, United's defence looked to be in for a tough and busy afternoon.

Sheffield United: Brown, Badger, Hemsley, Eddy, Colquhoun, Franks, Woodward, Speight, Dearden, Currie, Field. Substitute: France
Ipswich Town: Sivell, Burley, Mills, Talbot, Hunter, Beattie, Hamilton, Viljoen, Johnson, Whymark, Lambert. Substitute: Woods
Referee: Mr J. Humpty
Attendance: 17,963

Given the victory over Newcastle in midweek, the attendance again shocked the United board: gates were well short of 20,000 and unlikely to ease the financial pressures on the club. Yet the stay-away fans were to miss a real footballing treat as both sides served up a feast of fine passing football, with the emphasis on attacking enterprise. Making the early running, the visitors showed just why they were top of the table, but with Colquhoun and the superb Colin Franks dominant at the back, strikers Johnson and Whymark found clear opportunities difficult to come by, and it was the Blades who created the first real chances through Alan Woodward and Mick Speight, although neither was able to convert. With the match finely balanced, two goals in a minute put the Blades firmly in charge.

After 34 minutes Alan Woodward received the ball in the Ipswich box and, although seemingly shackled by the visitors' centre-half, sold him a dummy and struck a fierce shot at goal. Full-back Mick Mills, racing back to cover, was aghast as Woodward's shot, beating Sivell, struck the inside of the post, rebounded out and off the incoming full-back and into the back of the net. The Blades were a goal to the good and within a minute they had their second. Mick Speight, in possession, raced down the left and delivered a cross into the

Tony Field, hero against Ipswich, in action later in the season against Wolves.

Ipswich area. Billy Dearden, racing in, just failed to divert the ball towards goal, but in the mêlée of players around him, the ball somehow found its way to Tony Field who, up in support, smashed home a first-time rising shot to make it 2–0.

Playing well, United went off to huge applause at half-time, well worth their lead. The fine attacking play continued into the second half. The return of Billy Dearden had certainly provided for a more potent attack, as Currie and Woodward were able to feed dangerous balls in behind the opposition defence for the centre-forward to run on to. In addition, Dearden had given Tony Field a new lease of life. Struggling for form since his transfer from Blackburn the previous March, Field found that Dearden's presence took pressure off himself. Billy's runs and hold-up play allowed Tony more time and space, and in this game he was revelling in the opportunity. Most importantly, after 58 minutes Field scored one of the greatest goals seen at Bramall Lane, one that would forever live in the memories of those lucky enough to see it. Picking up a pass from Woodward, just inside the Ipswich half and out on the left, Tony Field set off on an amazing run that saw him dribble past Kevin Beattie, Allan Hunter and George Burley. As he advanced to the outside of the Ipswich area, cutting inside towards goal, he wrong-footed another couple of defenders before curling the ball around goalkeeper Laurie Sivell and inside the far post to make it 3–0. When the crowd, seeming momentarily stunned by what Field had just achieved, realised what a magnificent goal had been scored, wild jubilation ensued. Don Revie, ex-Leeds United and now current England manager, who was present at the game, later declared that 'it was one of the finest goals I have ever seen.'

Well ahead, the Blades had the measure of their opponents, having scored three times against a defence who had conceded none in their previous four games. Nevertheless, both sides continued to press forward and Ipswich probably deserved their consolation goal after 78 minutes, even though Furphy was not happy with the loose marking that allowed Mick Lambert to continue his personal scoring run when he was given ample time and space to finish off Viljoen's free-kick. With the final whistle, however, both United's manager and their supporters were more than satisfied with a result that cemented United's positive start to the season.

The victory saw the local media attempting to fight against the lethargy and pessimism of the Blades supporters, who were continuing to stay away from the Lane in large numbers. The crowd was 'pathetic' according to the *Star's* Tony Pritchett, while Benny Hill of the *Telegraph* noted that 'if Saturday's thrashing of Ipswich, one of the country's leading teams, does not silence some of the critics and chasten some of the moaners, Sheffield United might as well pack in and turn the ground into allotments!' With Don Revie adding his belief that the match was a 'great advertisement for English football', the hope was that the fans would return in larger numbers.

Importantly, the game had seen the return of Billy Dearden, who had provide much-needed experience and, hopefully, goals to come in the future. Dearden's return had also shown that Tony Field was not a foolish signing. Ken Furphy had paid Blackburn a substantial fee of £76,666 for his services, yet the forward had been disappointing and, as a result, had become something of a target for the Bramall Lane hecklers. After the game, Field acknowledged that his form had been 'in and out' and his poor scoring record entitled the fans to criticise him. Nevertheless, he continued, 'I've never stopped trying...[and] I trust I have now proved to the fans that I'm worth the transfer fee and good enough to play in the First Division.' Ken Furphy, whose judgement had been called into question, clearly felt vindicated by the player's performance against Ipswich, but also acknowledged that the return of Dearden had facilitated the improvement, 'I think he should share all the credit...[Dearden allowed] Field to play further forward, instead of leaving some of his energy in our own half.'

The game certainly proved a turning point for Tony Field and cemented his place in the side for the rest of the season. The attendance figures, however, did not see the kind of improvements envisaged by the board until far later in the season. Many fans remained unconvinced about United's prospects and the average gate remained around the 20,000 mark.

Tottenham Hotspur 1–3 Sheffield United Division One

18 January 1975

Following their excellent victory over Ipswich, the Blades went on a good run that saw them stay in the top six throughout the following month. A morale-boosting 1–0 defeat of Liverpool in front of 29,443 at Bramall Lane on 28 September was a particular highlight. The First Division was proving unusually competitive that season. With a number of sides showing the capacity to become title contenders, the top spot changed hands regularly. United were to effectively remain in the top 10 until the end of November, further confounding the doubters among their own supporters who were convinced that the club would be sucked into a relegation struggle. The Blades lost some momentum in December, however, suffering successive away defeats against Manchester City, Queen's Park Rangers and Middlesbrough. Yet prior to the game at White Hart Lane, the Blades had gone three games unbeaten, with two home draws in the League against Arsenal and Manchester City and a third-round FA Cup victory over Second Division Bristol City. The ship had been steadied and the Blades were looking forward to taking on their London hosts before the BBC's *Match of the Day* cameras.

United went into the match in 14th position with 25 points from 25 games; Spurs, having played a game more, were two places behind with 23 points. Spurs had a talented squad containing many experienced, expensive and high-profile players: 'keeper Pat Jennings, left-back Cyril Knowles (of *Nice One, Cyril* pop fame), Welsh centre-half Mike

England, Steve Perryman in midfield, World Cup winner Martin Peters, John Duncan and recent signing from Glasgow Rangers, Alfie Conn. As a result, the Tottenham fans were disappointed with the season they had experienced so far. They had already lost 11 League games, had been dumped out of the League Cup 4–0 at home by Middlesbrough back in September and had lost 1–0 to Second Division Nottingham Forest in an FA Cup third-round replay just 10 days ago. Some confidence and optimism had been restored, however, with a thumping 5–0 League victory against Newcastle at St James' Park the previous Saturday. New signing Alfie Conn had hit a hat-trick in the game. The Spurs match programme was, therefore, hopeful that 'our marksmanship will reach a comparable level in today's match'.

Tottenham's manager, Terry Neill, had no injury worries going into the game and, like Ken Furphy, was able to select an unchanged starting line up. Due to an ankle injury to Terry Nichol though, Steve Cammack took over on the United substitute's bench.

Tottenham Hotspur: Jennings, Kinnear, Knowles, Beal, England, Naylor, Neighbour, Perryman, Conn, Peters, Duncan. Substitute: Pratt

Sheffield United: Brown, Badger, Hemsley, Eddy, Colquhoun, Franks, Woodward, Bradford, Dearden, Currie, Field. Substitute: Cammack

Referee: Mr T. Spencer

Attendance: 15,812

Heavy, incessant rain in London on Saturday morning meant that the game was in serious doubt. Referee Mr Spencer carried out two pitch inspections at 1.30pm and 2pm before finally giving the go-ahead. It was perhaps a surprising decision given that the rain continued to fall throughout the afternoon, and although White Hart Lane had recently had a new drainage system installed, it was unable to stop the pitch from turning into something of a quagmire.

Right from the start water splashed up from the pitch as the players moved around, and the ball frequently skidded and bounced awkwardly. Players were finding it difficult to keep their balance and Mr Spencer soon awarded free-kicks against Tottenham's Mike England and then United's Ted Hemsley, as they both found it difficult to keep their balance and impeded their opponents. Yet players from this era were used to performing on difficult pitches and, gradually acclimatising as best they could, they got on with making the best of it. Ted Hemsley and Spurs' Martin Peters caused hilarity among the crowd as they slid together for several yards through the mud and water.

Such conditions meant that both defences had to be on their mettle, with the ball likely to skip through or hold up, thus providing an advantage to both sides' nippy forwards. In the opening minutes Woodward was almost put through by Franks' clever pass, only to be

Jim Brown who performed heroics in the United goal at White Hart Lane.

caught marginally offside, and then Mike England stuck out a long leg to cut out a ball that threatened to put Tony Field in the clear. Alfie Conn, hat-trick hero of the previous week and making his home debut, then thrilled the fans as he set off on an intricate dribble that threatened to have the Blades in trouble, only for him to be crowded out and ultimately dispossessed by the United defence. The Scot was proving to be a real danger and when, lurking in an offside position, a defensive deflection played him in on goal, his shot was only cleared off the line by Hemsley's heroic last-gasp slide through the mud.

Not to be outdone, the Blades responded with their own pressure, securing four corners in quick succession, yet unable to make 'keeper Pat Jennings work on any of them. The difficulties the goalkeepers could be put under, however, were clearly shown when, diving to save a shot, Jennings' momentum took the ball out for a corner as he slid through the mud and over the goalline.

Towards half-time a competitive game seemed to be tipping slightly in favour of the home team. Hemsley was forced into tripping Terry Naylor just outside the box but, fortunately for the Blades, the free-kick was wasted. Then the alert Jim Brown was quickly off his line to clear a through ball that had put John Duncan in on goal. In fact, Brown's performance so far was indeed impressive. Alert to every danger, he was particularly reliable in his handling, holding on to the wet, greasy and muddy ball as Spurs played a succession of high crosses into the area, hoping to force a mistake from the Blades' 'keeper. Jennings, too, was equally alert, beating Tony Field to a through ball and smashing it clear from outside the area. The Spurs 'keeper, however, was thoroughly beaten by the United man on the stroke of half-time, as the ball was chipped into the area and Field, making a mockery of the conditions, brilliantly pulled it down with his back to goal and, in one moment, swivelled and fired in a shot that thundered against the top of the bar and out to safety.

Off the hook, Spurs started the second half strongly. Duncan put in a good header that was just wide, and Conn tried a spectacular, acrobatic overhead-kick that, thanks to the conditions, failed to come off. After 51 minutes the home side took the lead. Conn, in midfield, sent a great pass out to full-back Cyril Knowles out on the left, who sent the ball into the United area. It seemed to offer little in the way of danger, but took a deflection and then stuck in the mud. John Duncan, refusing to look a gift horse in the mouth, reacted quickest, turning to hit a low shot past Jim Brown's despairing dive into the back of the net. Spurs, their tails up, almost got another as Naylor fired in a good cross, but Duncan could only head it straight at Brown. But from this point on it was the Blades who seized the initiative. Effectively, the goal had the effect of lifting United's resolve. 'We quickened it all up', noted Furphy after the game and, although Terry Neill later blasted his team's complacency after taking the lead, his complaints unfairly detract from the fact that the Blades played some scintillating football in the final 22 minutes.

The equalising goal, on 68 minutes, began with David Bradford hitting a first-time cross into the Spurs box, where Tony Field, a predator in the midst of the Spurs defence, diverted it towards goal. Jennings, wrong-footed by right-back Joe Kinnear's deflection, was unable to grasp hold of the shot and as the ball trickled out of his grasp, Tony Currie was on hand to knock it over the line. With the Blades now pressing, the Spurs defence came under increasing pressure, but as the minutes ticked away, it did not seem as if the Blades would score again. With four minutes to go, however, the away team produced a move of stunning proportions as they swept the ball quickly from one end of the field to the other to take the lead. The ball began with 'keeper Jim Brown, who fed Tony Currie, who knocked out a pass to Len Badger on the right. The full-back then pushed the ball up to Tony Field who delivered a superb ball into the Spurs box, where Keith Eddy, at the end of a surging supporting run from the middle of the park, arrived to hook the ball past Jennings. Keith Eddy's mud-splattered kit, his dirty face lit up by a beaming smile and congratulated by his delighted colleagues, was to cut a striking picture on that evening's *Match of the Day*. So impressive was this true team goal, that it was to win the Goal of the Month award for January.

With Spurs effectively beaten, the Blades still were not finished, and two minutes later they had their third goal. Tony Currie, increasingly dominant in the centre of midfield, delivered a slide-rule pass for Alan Woodward, who had beaten the offside trap, to race on to and clear of the Spurs defence. As Pat Jennings advanced to narrow the angle, Woodward calmly picked his spot and struck the ball powerfully past the Irish international 'keeper and into the net.

It had been a brilliant United performance. Benny Hill of the *Telegraph* concluded that 'There was an abundance of courage and determination. There was defensive strength when Tottenham pressurised; there was attacking flair when the scales tilted United's way, and two of their goals were certainly from the top locker.'

The game was certainly important for the Blades' season. Although the club were knocked out of the FA Cup at Aston Villa 4–1 the following week, League form continued to take an upturn, and a team that many supporters had shown little faith in began to find itself taken far more seriously after their superb display at White Hart Lane was shown on *Match of the Day*. The team also seemed to be clicking, and the absence of serious injuries or suspensions meant that the side was now fairly settled with very few changes needing to be made. In their next seven games the Blades won four, drew two and lost just once – against Burnley. By early March, therefore, the team found itself back in the top 10 with realistic aspirations of making it into Europe.

Sheffield United 3–2 West Ham United Division One

22 March 1975

As the West Ham match approached, the Blades were on their best run since Ken Furphy had taken over the manager's job 15 months before. They had lost only once in their last 10 League games, had won three out of their four last away fixtures and were six points behind leaders Everton with a game in hand. With nine games still to go, Furphy was upbeat. In an interview with the *Sheffield Telegraph* prior to the game, his confidence in his players knew no bounds: 'People have been talking about Sheffield United getting into the UEFA Cup next season. That means finishing among the leaders. If we can beat West Ham, I don't see why we can't talk in terms of the European Cup.' In effect, Furphy had not given up on the fact that if the Blades could maintain their consistency in a season where all the leading teams were taking points off each other, just maybe they could finish top of the pile at the end of the season.

A campaign that had started with a general sense of gloom was now unexpectedly threatening to develop into something very exciting. The strength of United's achievement was outlined by Jonathan Lang and Michael Morris of the *Sheffield Telegraph*, who noted that 'United's bold challenge for Leeds United's title is made against a background of poor attendances, too few First Division-class players in reserve and not enough money in the bank to assemble a galaxy of stars.' Some great news for Blades fans had been the recent announcement by chairman John Hassall that star asset Tony Currie would not be sold to help finance the South Stand. This was particularly reassuring; Furphy had taken the captaincy off 'TC' at the start of February, handing it to Keith Eddy, due to the belief that the extra responsibility was affecting the midfield maestro's performances. Currie had responded magnificently, having taken the decision well and putting in some brilliant performances that showed he was back to his best.

United had shown their resilience in the previous game against Liverpool at Anfield. They had defended solidly, yet on the counter-attack they had created four excellent chances which, unfortunately, they had been unable to convert. Nevertheless, they had come away with a goalless draw and increased credibility. The Anfield trip had seen Ted Hemsley miss his first game of the season, however – replaced by utility man David Bradford – and Billy Dearden come off injured after half-time. Neither expected to be fit for the West Ham game, in fact Hemsley's foot injury was to keep him out for the rest of the season, so Bradford continued at left-back and Steve Cammack was brought in to replace Dearden up front.

West Ham also had their injury worries. Captain Keith Robson and Billy Bonds were still out injured, and top scorer Billy Jennings was in doubt until being passed fit just before the game. Already in the FA Cup semi-final – they were to go on and win the Cup – West Ham were just two points behind the Blades, and manager John Lyall was determined that the hunt for a European place would be vigorously pursued through the League. The West Ham boss declared, 'Saturday's match is vital because we must keep our impetus going. Both teams have a lot to fight for this season and our team must remain in the right mood.' Promising for the fans was that Lyall declared that his team's intention was to play an open and attacking game.

The match was the first at Bramall Lane to be sponsored, a new avenue that United were pursuing to raise income. The sponsors were J.W. Gilder Ltd, Volkswagen and Audi dealers. As part of the pre-match entertainment, a welly-throwing contest took place, in which competitors from the supporters of both sides threw a size-8 regulation wellington, discus style, as far as they could.

Sheffield United: Brown, Badger, Bradford, Eddy, Colquhoun, Flynn, Woodward, Speight, Cammack, Currie, Field.
West Ham United: Day, Coleman, Lampard, McDowell, T. Taylor, Locke, Jennings, Paddon, A. Taylor, Brooking, Gould.
Referee: Mr J. Taylor
Attendance: 25,527

It was pleasing to the team and directors to see an attendance 5,000 up on the previous two home games, a reflection of a growing belief in the players. The BBC's recognition that

United were genuine European contenders was reflected in the fact that the *Match of the Day* cameras were present to capture the action – the first time they had been to the Lane that season.

True to John Lyall's word, the visitors came determined to attack and, with the Blades in a similar mood, the match got off to a cracking start. In the very first minute West Ham 'keeper Mervyn Day's long kick found Bobby Gould, who sent in a curling shot from the left that was successfully held by Blades 'keeper Jim Brown. After five minutes the visitors almost had the lead, as striker Alan Taylor allowed a long clearance to run on, collected the ball, turned Keith Eddy and fired in a powerful low drive that Brown superbly palmed around the post for a corner. Three minutes later the lively West Ham side did take the lead. John McDowell and Alan Taylor's teamwork saw McDowell racing on the overlap, receiving the ball and sending over a cross, which Bobby Gould headed firmly past Brown to make it 1–0.

Though stunned, the Blades hit back immediately. Currie played the ball to Woodward, whose goal-bound shot was blocked, the ball falling for Steve Cammack, whose own strike hit the post and rolled agonisingly along the line, only for Tony Currie, who had continued on into the box, to tap the ball home. Referee Mr Taylor, surrounded by West Ham players, dismissed their claims that he was offside. It was Currie's 50th League goal for the Blades on his 300th League and Cup appearance for the club.

The Blades were now producing some fine attacking play. Currie and Badger played neatly together, with Badger's resulting drive just over the top, and then some magic from Currie saw a cheeky backheel open up a shooting opportunity for Cammack, whose fierce drive brought a flying save from Day. Yet West Ham were always dangerous, and after 29 minutes they again had the lead, the result of an uncharacteristic error from Jim Brown. An overhead-kick from Billy Jennings speculatively launched the ball towards United's

That classic 'TC' moment. The 'quality goal by a quality player' secures victory against the Hammers.

goal. Brown seemed to have it covered, but inexplicably the ball slipped through his hands, over his shoulder and into the net. It meant that the Blades would again have to come from behind if they were going to win the game. Continuing to attack strongly, the Blades continued to make chances but when they went in at half-time, they were still trailing, as Flynn, Cammack and Currie all missed opportunities to level the game.

There was a real dynamic to United's performance, however, and within a minute of the restart they were desperately unlucky not to equalise. Woodward swung in a great cross from the right and Tony Field, flinging himself at the ball, was a whisker away from converting. Two minutes later West Ham actually had the ball in the net, but Mr Taylor adjudged that Gould had fouled Brown and the goal was disallowed. After 57 minutes the Blades did score and had their equaliser. It was a brilliant flowing move that saw Brown throw the ball out to Cammack on the right, who then hit a precise ball over the centre of the West Ham defence. Alan Woodward, running through in typical fashion, took the ball past one defender and then fired the ball past Day to make it 2–2. A splendid goal, it was worthy of being the landmark 1000th post-war Division One goal scored by the Blades. Back on terms, United were simply irresistible, producing some of the finest attacking fooball they had played in years. It was not all one-way traffic, however, and West Ham, prompted by England midfielder Trevor Brooking and with the dangerous pairing of Bobby Gould and Taylor up front, were always a threat.

After 70 minutes Keith Eddy's long clearance found Woodward, who beat two defenders and pushed the ball out to Cammack clear on the right. The young striker powered in a shot, but was extremely unlucky to see it come back off the bar with Day successfully beaten. Back came West Ham as Alan Taylor took advantage of Mick Speight's poor backpass to race through on Brown, only for United's Scottish 'keeper to make amends for his earlier blunder by bravely smothering the ball at Taylor's feet. United's response came as Tony Currie dribbled past two players before crashing a thunderous shot against the bar – another let off for 'keeper Mervyn Day.

There was no stopping 'TC' after 79 minutes, however. Alan Woodward rescued the ball from going out near the halfway line and fed Currie. 'TC' now advanced towards the West Ham goal, jinking and feinting this way and that, seeing the West Ham defender retreat before him. On the edge of the area, with Mervyn Day wrong-footed by his movements, Currie hit a low left-foot shot into the bottom corner of the net at the Shoreham Street end and went to take the adulation of his adoring fans. Played and replayed on television, the immortal words 'A quality goal by a quality player' have stayed in the memory of all Blades fans of that era: the goal that defines the magic that is 'TC'.

A minute later Currie had another magnificent effort superbly turned over the bar by Day. Cammack also went close to scoring, and Badger became the third United player to hit the bar as his shot also rebounded to safety.

It had been a tremendous game and had reinforced United's European aspirations. Eighth in the First Division, the Blades were now five points behind leaders Everton with a game in hand. Yet the competitive nature of the League was illustrated by the fact that there were 11 teams behind the leaders, all bunched within a five-point span. Even more significant in terms of Sheffield football was that, with Wednesday having an extremely poor season and looking destined for relegation to the Third Division, the Blades seemed to have become established firmly as the city's leading football club.

The game will ultimately be remembered for the genius of Currie. The *Telegraph*'s Keith Farnsworth, assessing his performance, declared, 'TC is just magic. If he goes on playing like this, England manager Don Revie just can't ignore him, and Harold (the voice in the main stand) will not take umbrage anymore when I mention TC in the same breath as Jimmy ("Sir James", insists Harold) Hagan.'

Farnsworth's reference was to the fact that the new England boss had declared that he would not pick 'flair' players like Currie, Stan Bowles or Rodney Marsh; Revie wanted those with 100 per cent application. It was an accusation – a lack of application and failure to always play to instructions – that centred on Currie, but it was mostly unjustified and unfair. In 'TC' a manager got genius, the ability to do the unexpected and turn a game on its head, the very quality international football cried out for. Furthermore, Farnsworth ackknowledged the generation gap within United's supporters. It was divided over who was the better player, Hagan or Currie. Given that most of the youngsters had never seen 'James' play, and many of their elders refused to ackknowledge that 'modern' football was 'proper' football, the debate could perhaps never be objectively resolved.

The last word on 'TC' is best left to West Ham manager John Lyall, who declared after the game, 'Currie was absolutely tremendous. I could not wish to see a better midfield display than that.'

Everton 2–3 Sheffield United
Division One

19 April 1975

United's title aspirations effectively disappeared over the next four games, as they were unable to secure the wins to put real pressure on the top position. Results were indeed creditable: a 2–2 draw at Coventry was followed by a controversial one-goal defeat to Arsenal at Highbury. Returning to the Lane, the Blades drew 1–1 with Leeds and then effectively ended Stoke's Championship ambitions by beating them 2–0. The Blades had played well in all four games and deserved more points, but nevertheless were still strongly in the hunt for a European place, and the attendances against Leeds (38,442) and Stoke (33,255) were a cause of much satisfaction for the United board. Derby were now top on 51 points and Everton second on 49 points. Both teams had just two games to play and it was clear that Everton had to beat United if they were to retain their now slim chances of becoming champions. The Blades, back in eighth place with 43 points, had the advantage of having two games in hand. It was also clear that United, like their opponents, had to win the game to keep their season alive.

Approaching the game, both camps were extremely complimentary about one another. Ken Furphy dismissed the accusations levelled at Everton that they were too negative and defensive, criticism that had continued to mount as Everton had slipped from the top spot with recent defeats against weaker opposition in Luton and Carlisle. Furphy believed that Everton, having made some expensive signings in Martin Dobson and Bob Latchford and introduced younger players like Ken McNaught, Peter Scott, George Telfer and 'keeper Dai Davies, were in a transitional period. In this he saw similarities with United's own situation. Dismissing accusations of negativity concerning the Toffees, Furphy pointed out how Everton had made a magnificent comeback against the Blades at Bramall Lane on 12 October to come back from 2–0 down to secure a draw. Considering them one of the best attacking teams to come to the Lane, Furphy expected a tough test at Goodison Park.

The Everton match programme was equally generous with their praise for the Blades. Special plaudits were handed out to Keith Eddy and Tony Currie, the latter having 'found the form which promised to make him an England regular last season'. Eddy, meanwhile, was praised for his 'tactical leadership qualities' displayed since he took over the team captaincy. Blades boss Ken Furphy was quoted as saying, 'Keith is more than a good captain, he is a brilliant player and tactician. The trouble is, I want two Keith Eddys in my side: one in the back four and another in midfield.' Most of all, however, the Blades were praised in the match programme for being a 'real team', a club that had confounded the critics and the pundits who had tipped them for relegation. Furphy had continued the good work of John Harris in 'bringing players out of the lower divisions and welding them into a neat, skilful First Division unit.' Effectively, United's success had confounded the general wisdom that spending vast sums on new talent was the way to success.

Going into the game, United, after an injury scare to Keith Eddy, were unchanged. Everton were missing Mike Lyons and Steve Sargeant through injury. Recent signing David Smallman, £75,000 from Wrexham, was brought in for his home debut.

Everton: Davies, Bernard, Clements, Buckley, Kenyon, Hurst, Jones, Dobson, Latchford, Smallman, Pearson. Substitute: Telfer

Sheffield United: Brown, Badger, Bradford, Eddy, Colquhoun, Flynn, Woodward, Speight, Dearden, Currie, Field. Substitute: Franks

Referee: Mr W. Gow

Attendance: 38,348

A morning of rain was replaced by fine and sunny weather As the match kicked-off, however, there was still plenty of moisture on what proved to be a tricky pitch. The importance of the game was clearly evident from the start and it was the home side who seized the initiative, creating the early pressure and good chances. Bob Latchford headed narrowly wide of the post, while Jim Brown made some smart saves from Latchford, Smallman and Dobson. Keith Eddy, playing as a sweeper, was marshalling United's defence superbly and when Currie raced away down the left and cut the ball back for Bradford to test Everton 'keeper Dai Davies, Everton knew that they were in for a difficult game.

Yet, continuing to dictate the pace of the game, the home side's pressure began to mount as the United defence were forced into a number of fouls around their own area. One free-kick saw Latchford put in a strong downward header, but fortunately Jim Brown was equal to it. Again the Blades gained some respite as Currie produced a good run and fed the ball into Mick Speight who, from the edge of the Everton penalty area, ballooned the ball over the bar. With Everton returning to the attack, the United defence found itself in danger of being overwhelmed, and after 20 minutes there were strong shouts for a penalty against Keith Eddy, but referee Mr Gow declared that the ball had struck Eddy's thigh rather than his hand.

Four minutes later the home pressure finally told as David Smallman, back to goal, picked up a loose ball, turned and smashed a ferocious shot beyond Brown's despairing dive into the top corner of the net. It was a brilliant goal to mark the player's home debut and it duly sent Goodison Park into raptures. Buoyed by the goal, Everton, confident and aggressive, continued to press against the Blades' defence, the visitors finding it hard to make any real headway against their opponents.

After 30 minutes the Blades found themselves with a real opportunity to get back into the game. Awarded a free-kick outside the Everton box on one of their, by now, rare forays forward, Tony Currie touched the ball off to Len Badger, who sent in a thunderous shot which thumped against the post with Davies completely beaten. The ball rebounded out and was scrambled away by the defence and Everton were immediately on the attack. To cover his position, Badger raced back down the pitch and, finding himself caught the wrong side of Everton's Jim Pearson in the area, brought down the midfielder from behind as he prepared to shoot. Referee Gow had no hesitation in pointing to the penalty spot and Gary Jones stepped up to plant the ball beyond Brown to make it 2–0. In danger of being put out of the game completely, the Blades somehow managed to hang on in the final minutes. Bob Latchford spurned the chance of putting the game beyond the visitors when, with only Brown to beat, he could only knock the ball wide of the post.

Everton's first-half performance had been superb, the Goodison crowd cheering them off the pitch at half-time. Yet, just three minutes after the restart, the Blades stunned the home support by grabbing a goal back. Bernard conceded a free-kick following a foul on Tony Field. From the kick, ex-Wednesday left-back Dave Clements sliced the ball out for a corner. Woodward delivered it into the box where Keith Eddy stooped to head it past Davies from a few yards out. Eddy's clinical finish was the signal for the Blades to take control of the game, similar to the way their opponents had dominated proceedings in the first half. Currie and Dearden played a neat one-two that almost put Billy in on goal, but for a last-ditch challenge by Roger Kenyon. Woodward went down in the box, but no penalty was given and, as the hour mark approached, it seemed that Everton had weathered United's pressure, and Currie showed signs of frustration as he was booked for dissent.

With the play evenly balanced, it seemed that the next goal would be crucial. After 73 minutes Len Badger, who was making increasing forays down the right flank, again got down the wing and delivered a cross into the Everton box. David Bradford, up in support, went for the ball with Dai Davies. Everton's 'keeper failed to hold on to the ball which fell to the ground and Billy Dearden reacted quickest to poke the ball home for the equaliser. The goal was a crushing blow for Everton's players and fans, who could see that their title hopes were now fast disappearing.

It was the Blades who continued to push forward, positively providing the belief, effort and commitment to secure the two points. It was not surprising, therefore, when five minutes from time the Blades scored the winner. Len Badger sent Tony Field away on the right. Field then delivered a great cross into the centre, where Tony Currie, who had run powerfully from midfield, controlled the ball and struck it past Davies to make it 3–2.

It had been a fantastic performance by the Blades, the game a reversal of the events at Bramall Lane back in October, where it had been the Merseysiders who had recovered from a first-half pounding to record a stunning comeback. Having ended Everton's title hopes – only Ipswich now had a mathematical chance of catching champions-elect Derby – United's own European prospects were still alive. Having moved up to seventh place, the Blades were three points behind Stoke in fifth, the minimum position they would have to reach to qualify. The Blades had three fixtures left and one, or two, games in hand on their rivals. The difficult run-in saw them unbeaten: a 1–1 draw at Chelsea, followed by a thumping 4–0 win at home against Leicester and a final day goalless draw away to Birmingham, was an excellent finish to the season. Sadly, however, it proved not quite enough to secure the prize. The Blades finished sixth on 49 points, just four points behind champions Derby and missing out on a European place. Nevertheless, United had completed the season on a real high. No one had expected them to challenge for honours and now expectation levels rose for the new season.

Match 20

Sheffield United 1–1 Derby County
Division One

16 August 1975

On 16 August 1975 United began the season at Bramall Lane against Derby County, the current champions, with 31,316 attending. All Blades were highly optimistic. The team had finished only four points behind the Rams and the new South Stand was completed. The Blades had a four-sided ground for the first time ever, with the promise of increased revenue from the 8,000 extra seats. Manager Ken Furphy saw it as 'a symbol of the strides we are attempting to make into the future'. With United's worldwide profile being raised by close-season tours that had taken in Kuwait, New Zealand and Tunisia, Furphy added that the club had never been able to 'push forward into a new season on such a high note'. Even the new Bramall Lane pitch, with its new irrigation system, looked greener than ever!

'Welcome to the new Bramall Lane…it's simply humming…the players feel it and accept the challenge', declared the match programme. Yet a note of caution was also sounded. 'A lot of money has been spent on a gamble in which we all have a part to play…if the attendances are worthy of Division One, our board can continue its forward thinking.' Indeed, it was a gamble; a large loan had been secured to build the stand and the team needed success, and with it the high attendances, to pay off the interest. The shareholders in the recent Annual General Meeting had been informed that there were bank debts of £850,000 that had to be cleared in five years, 'a mammoth tax, but one that is under firm control', declared chairman John Hassall. It was a tall order for the Blades, but, following

A feature in the club programme extolling the virtues of United's EDS club. An innovative attempt to provide a secure football experience for younger supporters.

Hello, lads and lasses!
I see the juvenile enclosure is getting fuller and during the Arsenal game you really made yourselves heard. Well done!
Mr. Furphy has promised to show his photographs and those of the players taken on the New Zealand tour. Watch the Press for the date.
The ball for today's game has been donated by all of you. Thanks a lot.
If you still have sponsored swim money, please hand it in as soon as possible.

Girls: Meet at the Odeon Cinema, Sunday, 31st August at 9.45 a.m. to proceed to the Sheffield Show.
There are still a few seats left for Liverpool and you can also book for the West Ham game before or after today's game in the Souvenir Shop.
Remember, all of you—support your team.
UnitED UnitED

the controversial sale of Geoff Salmons at the end of the 1973–74 season – ostensibly to help pay for the new stand – he reassured shareholders that 'the short-term financial problems could be resolved by selling players, but the board have elected to pursue a new policy in attempting to provide more success on the field of play.' Reading between the lines, United's survival and development as a First Division club hinged on the players gaining success on the field and raising attendances and money through the turnstiles.

Financial constraints meant that United had only brought in one new signing, centre-forward Chris Guthrie from Southend for a club record fee of £87,222. Tall and strong, it was hoped that Guthrie would add power to the forward line and finish off the crosses that would be provided by Tony Currie and Alan Woodward. Chairman John Hassall indicated that Guthrie's signing was a vindication of the ambition of his board of directors. An examination of Derby County's playing squad told something of a different story, however.

It is difficult to recall just how powerful a side Derby were in the early 1970s. Their renaissance in the late 1960s was, of course, down to Brian Clough, who took them from being a poor Second Division side to English Champions in 1971–72. Clough had left in October 1973. It was a move he later regretted, claiming in his autobiography *Walking on Water* that if he had stayed he could have turned them into a club as big as Manchester United. His first team captain, Dave Mackay, had stepped into the breach and, using the basis of Clough's team and some shrewd acquisitions of his own – Francis Lee, Bruce Rioch (1975 PFA Player of the Year) and Henry Newton – had guided the Rams to the title in 1974–75. Derby's ambition in these years was shown by their large outlay in transfer fees: David Nish for £225,000, Colin

Chris Guthrie was a key signing for the 1975–76 season. Unfortunately, he proved unable to fulfil manager Ken Furphy's expectations.

Todd for £170,000, Rioch for £170,000, Lee for £100,000 and Charlie George for £100,000. Furthermore, an additional £40,000 was shared by the 1974–75 squad, in addition to their bonuses throughout the season. This was financial power that the Blades just could not match and indicated just how well United had done to finish just four points short of the champions at the end of the previous season.

Derby, who the previous week had won the Charity Shield against West Ham at Wembley, would be going into the game with Jefff Bourne replacing the suspended Kevin Hector up front. With Roger Davies unavailable through injury, they also had Charlie George making his League debut. The Blades were giving Chris Guthrie his League debut too, but they would be without the suspended Tony Currie and Eddie Colquhoun. Currie's replacement was Terry Garbett, a hard-working and committed player, but certainly not one of consistent First Division quality. Garbett was an indication of the worrying lack of top-quality cover in United's small playing squad.

Sheffield United: Brown, Badger, Bradford, Eddy, Franks, Flynn, Woodward, Speight, Guthrie, Garbett, Field. Substitute: Cammack
Derby County: Boulton, Thomas, Nish, Rioch, McFarland, Todd, Newton, Gemmill, Lee, Bourne, George. Substitute: Hinton
Referee: Mr I. Smith
Attendance: 31,316

There was a pre-match entertainment to celebrate the opening of the new stand – music and marching by a jazz band and a special penalty-kick competition involving former players. Ex-Wednesday star Albert Broadbent, scoring six out of six, saw off the challenge of fellow Owl Redfern Froggatt and ex-Blades Harold Brook, Graham Shaw, Tommy Hoyland and Denis Finnegan. The supporters were in something of a carnival mood as the game got underway in glorious sunny weather.

Starting where they left off the season before, the Blades were quickly on the attack. In the first minute Guthrie's flick-on sent Alan Woodward away, his fierce shot rebounding off Derby 'keeper Colin Boulton's chest and gathered at the second attempt. A through ball from Badger again released 'Woody', but this time he pulled his shot just wide. At the other end, Derby attempted to hit back and Brown was tested by two crosses into the area from the Derby left. United's response was a fine counter-attacking move that saw Garbett shoot narrowly wide.

After 11 minutes, it was the visitors who had the chance to take the lead. Exerting pressure on the United goal, Derby gained a series of corners and, from the last of these, new boy Chris Guthrie handled the ball in the box to give away a penalty. The normally reliable Bruce Rioch stepped up confidently, but Jim Brown guessed right and did

A DAY TO REMEMBER
SATURDAY, 16th AUGUST, 1975

The opening of the new South Stand was graced by a fine match against the 1974-75 League Champions, Derby County.

A view of United's new South Stand, opened for the fixture against champions Derby.

magnificently to push the ball away. Fortune favoured United's 'keeper, however, as Francis Lee, following up on the rebound, shot against the post. Brown later revealed that his time with Rioch in the Scottish squad had given him an idea of where the Derby player would place his kick.

With both sides eager to attack, a series of opportunities came at both ends. Guthrie broke past Roy McFarland, but could only shoot over, and the England centre-half was forced to haul Woodward to the ground, receiving a booking, when he threatened to break clear. Derby, meanwhile, had a great chance to score as Charlie George allowed the ball to run through his legs, only for Rioch to shoot weakly at Brown. It was the Blades who were getting on top by half-time, however, as the Derby defence came under increasing pressure. Guthrie almost had a debut goal as he thundered a header, from Badger's cross, against the post with Boulton beaten, and United's centre-forward was denied a penalty when seemingly brought down by the 'keeper after he dropped Garbett's cross in the area.

The Blades continued to look dangerous after the break with Chris Guthrie having an excellent debut, creating problems for the central-defensive pairing of England internationals Colin Todd and Roy McFarland. The debutant was being warmly applauded by the Lane crowd, especially when he chased a ball from Tony Field, beat Todd and fired in a shot that had Boulton desperately scrambling across goal to keep out. Moments later Guthrie threatened again and he turned quickly in the box, only to be frustrated by Derby's 'keeper. With Keith Eddy composed and controlling the midfield, United were getting on top, yet with a side of Derby's quality they had to be alert to the counter-attack. A clear warning was given to them when David Nish sent in a shot that forced Brown into a good save. After 65 minutes the Blades finally got themselves in front. Alan Woodward, dribbling through the Derby defence, was into the area and in on goal, only to be bundled off the ball. Awarded a penalty, Keith Eddy calmly thumped the ball beyond Boulton's right hand to make it 1–0.

The goal was well-deserved and, as Derby attempted to get back on terms, it looked as if the Blades were completely in control. When Derby did threaten, Brown proved equal, especially when pulling off a smart save from Rioch. Yet as the game entered its final stages, the Blades were denied their win. With six minutes to go Nish crossed from the left and the ball broke to debutant Charlie George who, having had an ineffective game until this point, smashed an unstoppable volley past Brown to rescue a point.

Disappointed that they had been denied victory, Furphy, his players and supporters were buoyed by the excellent performance put in by the team. Benny Hill of the *Telegraph* agreed: 'Sheffield United started where they left off last season. Confident, compact and indeed at times a shade cocky, they deserved to win against new League champions.' There was a real sense of optimism following the game, a real belief that the Blades were establishing themselves as a top First Division side. Indeed, the performance had been achieved without the suspended Tony Currie and Eddie Colquhoun.

What followed, therefore, stunned Blades supporters. United went on a run of seven straight League defeats until finally defeating Burnley at the Lane on 23 September. Addressing the question of what had gone wrong, Furphy declared in the Burnley programme that injuries and loss of form had not helped and 'attempts to strengthen our squad to compensate were frustrated by our financial position. Our ability to sign players with proven track records is just not on and, therefore, we have to work with the fact that new signings are players from the lower divisions with ability.' In a sense, the loss of form

A new cartoon strip introduced into the programme at the start of the 1975–76 season. 'Billy of the Blades' was soon to be withdrawn, however, as unsuccessful as the team themselves. It clearly wasn't a time for humour!

of senior players hampered the ability of the younger, less experienced players to develop and, once on a bad run, pressure mounted on the players, so making it even more difficult to perform. In addition, as apathy began to set in among the supporters there was little chance of attaining the 30,000 average attendance essential to provide funds to strengthen the side; the signing of Cliff Calvert for just under £40,000 from York City prior to the Burnley game was a clear illustration of United's weak transfer policy.

With a win against Burnley, Furphy hoped it would provide a platform to restore the players' confidence and the manager reminded supporters, in the light of the recent barracking directed towards Mick Speight, that they too must stay solidly behind the players. Yet defeat in the following fixtures – 1–0 at home to Norwich in front of just 20,626 supporters and 2–0 at Birmingham – led to the board sacking Ken Furphy on 6 October.

The decision would prove to be premature and did not solve United's difficulties. Suggestions of a breakdown in the relationship between manager and chairman clearly did not help. The club were facing an incredibly difficult financial situation and Furphy's strategy of developing the youth system, after relegation and stabilisation of the club at a lower level, had every chance of eventually paying dividends. Furphy had clearly moulded a team that had massively overachieved in 1974–75 and was probably unfairly treated in not being allowed the time or the chance to rebuild. With hindsight, the board had every reason to regret their decision.

Norwich City 1–3 Sheffield United
Division One

3 April 1976

Ken Furphy was initially replaced on a caretaker basis by coach Cec Coldwell, who presided over two League defeats and elimination from the League Cup at the hands of Hull City, before United appointed Jimmy Sirrel as their new boss on 21 October. On the same day the United board received a written transfer request from Tony Currie. Sirrel had an impressive record in the lower divisions at Notts County, where he had achieved two promotions and got the club into the Second Division for the first time in 15 years on a shoestring budget. He was taking over in extremely difficult circumstances at Bramall Lane, however. In his first game in charge, the Blades went down by a single goal to Queen's Park Rangers at Loftus Road, yet the following week, 1 November, they fought back from two goals down to earn a draw against Manchester City, sparking hopes that Sirrel could inject some belief and improvement into the team. It was to prove a false hope, however, as the Blades were walloped 5–1 at Villa Park in their next fixture, with Aston Villa boss Ron Saunders claiming that it ought to have been 23–0!

Sirrel quickly brought in ex-Celtic legend Jimmy Johnstone – a free agent who had been playing in America – and young left-back Paul Garner for £59,555 from Huddersfield Town. But Johnstone proved to be a shadow of his former self – a gamble that did not pay off. Furthermore, it was apparent that Sirrel did not hit it off with his senior players and relations within the United camp were strained. Not surprisingly, United's prospects

Mrs Housley, the housekeeper, having prepared the meal, Mrs Sirrel, wife of the Sheffield manager, serves the young trialists who stayed at Moncrieffe House, United's resident accommodation for young players, at Easter.

continued to look gloomy, and the playing record under Sirrel was a complete disaster as the supporters had to wait another 19 League games following the Burnley match to win again, 2–1 against Aston Villa on 14 February 1976. The departure of senior players and the emphasis on youth did nothing to halt the decline.

When United travelled to Norwich on 3 April 1976 their relegation from Division One had been confirmed, following a five-goal thrashing at Tottenham the previous week. Having won just twice in 36 games and facing an in-form Norwich team, another profitless afternoon seemed to beckon. Nevertheless, a sizeable contingent of Blades fans had made

the trip to East Anglia, leading manager Jimmy Sirrel to declare this loyal support as 'one of the reasons why we will win in the end; these supporters are special.' Significantly, the Blades still had something to play for. The team needed to achieve an average of a point per game in their last six fixtures if they were to avoid registering the lowest First Division points total in history.

With the pressure to avoid relegation off, Sirrel chose the Norwich game to give 17-year-old centre-back Tony Kenworthy his League

United boss Jimmy Sirrel.

debut, and he continued with young Simon Stainrod, also 17, up front following his debut against Spurs the previous week. With Paul Garner having injured an ankle, the young left-back missed his first start since his transfer back in early November. As a result, Steve Goulding was switched from right to left full-back and Colin Franks from midfield to right-back. United's line up also saw the return of Mick Speight and David Bradford. Their return, following injury, would have a key impact on the Blades' performance. Norwich, safe from relegation fears in mid-table, had just achieved a morale-boosting 1–0 home victory against East Anglian rivals Ipswich Town. Strong at Carrow Road, they were particularly powerful up front: Ted MacDougall had scored 26 League and Cup goals; Martin Peters, World Cup winner and future Blade, was still a class act and had struck 13 times; Phil Boyer, who had recently won an England cap, had scored another nine. Against a solid First Division outfit, the Blades would clearly have their work cut out to get any type of result.

Norwich City: Keelan, Morris, Sullivan, McGuire, Davids, Powell, Miller, MacDougall, Boyer, Suggett, Peters.
Sheffield United: Brown, Franks, Goulding, Speight, Colquhoun, Kenworthy, Woodward, Stainrod, Guthrie, Currie, Bradford. Substitute: Flynn
Referee: Mr J. Homewood
Attendance: 19,218

The confirmation of their relegation seemed to free the blades from the tension and pressure of previous weeks, and the team started with fire and purpose. After just five minutes they were a goal to the good. Mick Speight and David Bradford combined down the left. The latter crossed into the centre, where Chris Guthrie lost his man to crash an unstoppable shot past City's 'keeper Kevin Keelan from 15 yards. On 22 minutes it was two. Bradford sent a pass into the path of Simon Stainrod, who fired home. It was a magnificent moment for Stainrod; his first League goal in just his second appearance. The Norwich fans could not believe what was happening – the division's 'whipping boys' were taking them to the cleaners! Incredibly, just before half-time, it was three. Tony Currie, out on the left touchline, crossed to Guthrie. The tall striker missed the ball completely, but wrong-footed Keelan, who could only watch as the ball landed inside the far post. Incredibly, this was Currie's first goal of the season.

A minute into the second half the Canaries finally hit back, with Phil Boyer heading in a Suggett corner at the far post. With renewed vigour, City continued to surge forward. Yet for once in this disastrous season, good fortune favoured the Blades. Twice they cleared off the line, Boyer chested the ball against the post and Ted MacDougall missed an open goal. Yet the Blades also defended tenaciously. Eddy did an excellent marking job on

SIMON STAINROD

TONY KENWORTHY

MacDougall, while young Tony Kenworthy effectively shackled England man Phil Boyer. Jim Brown also pulled off superb point-blank saves from Martin Peters and John Miller. With Currie showing his class in midfield, the Blades also remained dangerous on the break and were unlucky to have a Mick Speight strike ruled out for offside, after a brilliant solo run by Alan Woodward. When the final whistle went, the Blades, at the 19th time of asking, had scored their first away League win of the season.

It was a tremendous morale-boosting victory for United and their supporters, Jimmy Sirrel the recipient of praise from the travelling Blades, who sang *Nice One, Sirrel* at the end of the game – a play on the words of the Tottenham chart hit. The manager was delighted at the result, declaring, 'I think it's important you go down with style and some sort of future.' The future had been glimpsed at Carrow Road in the performances of Stainrod and Kenworthy, a couple of United's promising youngsters who were to stay in the team for the remainder of the season. Fortunately, the Blades avoided the unwanted distinction of achieving a record low points total as they won four and drew one of those final six games, including a pleasing 1–0 victory, courtesy of Alan Woodward's strike, at Yorkshire rivals Leeds United.

For hope for the future, United had to look no further than their competitors on the day, Norwich City. Bottom of the First Division table in 1973–74, the Canaries had gained instant promotion. As manager John Bond had noted in his programme notes, 'Perhaps we can offer some encouragement by pointing out that we went down – and bounced straight back again!' Yet Norwich were in a healthier financial position than the Blades and relegation had compounded United's problems. As Jimmy Sirrel noted in the Birmingham match programme on 4 May, the final game of the season, finances were 'a nightmare'. The First Division

Tony Field challenges Burnley's Alan Stevenson earlier in the season.

had meant that the club could budget on the basis of crowds coming to see the elite clubs of English football. With the Second Division beckoning, 'the home gate is in the balance and the away gate is, in many cases, almost non-existent'. At this time, clubs got a share of the gate in their away League fixtures, so United's relegation to a League of smaller, less supported clubs would clearly hurt. Yet Sirrel noted that, although it had been a difficult season personally for him – the failure of relegation and having to travel home for 40 hours a week – there was cause for optimism: the fans, who regardless of everything had been tremendous, and the youngsters.

It seemed that the board were putting their faith in the latter, the Birmingham programme declaring, 'We have faith in his [Mr Sirrel's] ability to develop our young players and to restore our former prestige. He has the full backing of the board of directors and he has our confidence.'

Sheffield United 1–1 Fulham
Division Two

16 October 1976

Visiting Bramall Lane, Fulham were not just the talk of the Second Division, but had also become the focus of attention for the whole football world. When millionaire Ernie Clay joined the Fulham board as an executive director on 2 August 1976, his intention was to help chairman Tommy Trinder 'make Fulham one of the outstanding clubs in the game.' Under Trinder, Fulham had strong connections with the showbiz world of entertainment, and Clay decided to inject star quality into the team's line up by the high-profile signings of George Best and Rodney Marsh from Los Angeles Aztecs and Tampa Bay Rowdies of the North American Soccer League. These two signings added to the presence of World Cup-winning skipper Bobby Moore, who was already at Craven Cottage and had skippered Fulham in the FA Cup Final of 1975. Best, the ultimate footballing genius, was a real gamble. Having walked out on Manchester United twice and played briefly for Stockport County in the Fourth Division prior to leaving for the USA, Fulham manager Alec Stock was not expecting a bed of roses. Reportedly, Best was on a match fee of £500 and the talented, extrovert Rodney Marsh was also a considerable investment.

Yet the signings had captured the imagination of football fans up and down the country. The financial outlay seemed justified to Clay, as a gate of over 21,000 watched the duo's first home game against Bristol Rovers on 4 September. This was over twice Fulham's average attendance in the previous season. To inspire the fans further, Best scored after just 71 seconds, although

Fulham only gained a 1–0 victory. Rodney Marsh famously said that English football in the late 1970s was becoming a 'grey game' played on 'grey days'. He believed that the razzmatazz of the NASL, with each game becoming a package of all-round entertainment, was the way forward. Certainly, the new Fulham side seemed to offer glamour through the presence of Moore, Best and Marsh. Fans all around the country responded positively to the new-look Fulham team, and attendances doubled wherever they played. Yet with this interest and excitement came an expectation that Fulham would deliver exciting displays. This was fine for Best and Marsh, who could do so, but more demanding for the ordinary members of the squad. Fulham boss Alec Stock quickly acknowledged that the difficulty was 'to turn entertainment into wins'.

Stock had worked long enough in the Second Division to know that it was a tough League and, coming to Bramall Lane, he declared, 'we won't have an easy task in Sheffield.' A glance at the League table showed that it was indeed a competitive division. Leaders Chelsea had 13 points from nine games and had already lost twice; Fulham and United both had nine points and were in mid-table.

After a shaky start to the season, United had stabilised to go on a run of seven League games unbeaten, although five of these fixtures had been drawn. This led Jimmy Sirrel to stress that United's youth development programme was starting to show dividends. In his article for the Fulham matchday programme, he noted how his appointment of Neville Briggs as chief scout back in January had enabled the club to utilise its considerable investment in youth development by identifying promising young talent outside, as well as within, the United area. Sirrel also noted how well the young players who had worked their way into the first team were performing. Referring to the 3–0 home victory over Carlisle on 11 September, Sirrel pointed out that the team had included Paul Garner, Tony Kenworthy, Steve Ludlam, Keith Edwards and John McGeady. Yet young players were prone to inconsistency and loss of form in their normal course of development, and Sirrel neglected to mention that United's unbeaten run had come to a crashing halt the previous week in their 6–1 reversal against Nottingham Forest at the City Ground on 9 October; Edwards, Garner, Ludlam and Kenworthy had all played in that fixture. Nevertheless, on a positive note, Tony Kenworthy, Simon Stainrod and Gary Hamson had all recently been invited to England youth trials at Lilleshal, a seeming vindication of the youth development programme.

Refusing to let his players be rattled by their big-name opponents, Sirrel, in his pre-match interviews, reminded the media that his team had just come down from the top flight and 'were playing against these sort of people every week…they are used to playing in front of bigger crowds than Fulham ever get.' It seemed that Sirrel did not approve of the 'Fulham Road show'. Team news for the Blades was promising; Alan Woodward, recovering from sore ribs, would be able to play and Jimmy Johnstone was back after missing three games through injury. Johnstone would replace young Keith Edwards. Mick Speight, who had returned against Sheffield Wednesday in a midweek County Cup victory following a cartilage operation, was available to take his place on the bench. John McGeady, however, had just had an X-ray on a troublesome knee and was unavailable.

For Fulham, the pleasing news for the fans going to the Lane was that the big two would play. George Best, fresh from his recall to the Northern Ireland team in their 2–2 midweek draw against Holland in Rotterdam, was in the team, as was Rodney Marsh, who had missed the last game due to an ankle injury.

Sheffield United: Brown, Franks, Garner, Flynn, Colquhoun, Calvert, Woodward, Johnstone, Guthrie, Ludlam, Hamilton. Substitute: Speight
Fulham: Mellor, Cutbush, Strong, Slough, Howe, Moore, Best, Evanson, Mitchell, Marsh, Barrett. Substitute: Bullivant
Referee: Mr J. Rice
Attendance: 28,792

The Best–Marsh factor again paid dividends, as United's gate was over 12,700 up on the previous highest attendance of the season. The crowd were still pouring in at kick-off and regional interest in the Fulham team was shown by the presence of Yorkshire TV, who were recording the match for their Sunday highlights show.

Ironically, as Best touched the ball in the opening stages, United's Kop jeered him, but he responded in typical fashion by sending a beautiful, long ball into the path of Les Barrett. Fortunately for the Blades, the Fulham man was unable to control it.

It was United who created the first chance. In the third minute Alan Woodward fed Chris Guthrie, who laid the ball across to Jimmy Johnstone. Unfortunately, the ball wobbled as the winger made contact and, from just a few yards out, the chance had gone. Fulham responded well to the scare and in the opening minutes it was Barrett, Marsh and Mitchell who were at the centre of their most-promising moves. Mitchell almost caught United's 'keeper, Jim Brown, out with a shot which dipped just over the bar, and Cliff Calvert blocked Marsh's goal-bound effort.

With Fulham beginning to dominate, the Blades struck back in a spectacular fashion. After 16 minutes United's own star, Alan Woodward, received the ball from Guthrie, went past Bobby Moore and thumped one of his trademark 'specials' past Mellor from the edge of the area. It was 1–0 to the Blades and, in the words of the *Green 'Un's* Tony Pritchett, 'the crowd, who had come to see Best, were suddenly chanting for Woodward.' Needing to respond, Best, up until then having a quiet game, began to prompt Fulham. With Marsh busy and skilful, the two men, ably supported by Mitchell, Slough and Evanston, began to exert real pressure on United's goal. Brown was relieved to see a Best shot, fired in after some mesmerising twists and turns in the United box, pass wide of his right-hand post, and Colin Franks was a real presence, blocking and clearing a succession of balls into the area. Having stuck to their defensive duties and having weathered the Fulham pressure, the Blades were unfortunate not to go further ahead on the stroke of half-time, when a fine shot by Chico Hamilton had Mellor thoroughly beaten but just cleared the bar.

The Blades, attacking the Kop, started the second half well, exerting early pressure and forcing a corner. Best, however, flitting in and out of the game, took advantage of a mistake by Garner to feed Les Strong, but the full-back shot straight at Brown. Yet 10 minutes into the second half Fulham were level with a goal that mirrored the quality of Woodward's. The ball started with goalkeeper Peter Mellor, who threw it out to Bobby Moore, who sent a great ball through the United defence. John Mitchell, out on the left, raced on to it and, with Brown coming out to narrow the angle, advanced towards the United area and fired a vicious shot across and beyond the Scottish 'keeper and into the corner of the net.

With the game now evenly balanced, both sides were looking for the win. While Best was being capably shackled by Calvert, ably supported by his colleagues, Johnstone was looking increasingly dangerous as he set about the Fulham defence. The Celtic legend, who had failed to show any real signs of greatness in his previous appearances, seemed to be inspired by the presence of Best and was having his best performance in a United shirt. Yet the Blades were unable to find any end product to their industry, and it was Fulham who, in the closing stages, went closest to victory. But the Blades' defence stuck to their task well and the game ended all square.

George Best and Rodney Marsh had certainly brought in the crowds and an extra £10,000, it was estimated, to the Sheffield kitty. Yet the two players had, to a degree, been controlled by a committed Blades performance, and the most impressive individuals on the pitch had been Alan Woodward and Jimmy Johnstone. Woodward's goal, recorded for posterity on television, was a reminder of how great a player he truly was and Johnson's performance, on this particular day, had put Best in the shade. Manager Jimmy Sirrel, taking the positives from the performance, noted that his team had strong personalities, too. More importantly, the crowd, following the disappointing result at Nottingham Forest the week before, were solidly behind the team. 'We thought the support was fantastic and if we get going, we know the city is with us,' remarked the Blades boss. Yet it was a season of transition and United's form was too inconsistent for them to ultimately become serious promotion contenders and build on the enthusiasm of the supporters at the Fulham game. The Blades would not better the crowd all season.

Following the Fulham game, the Blades lost at Charlton, but there then followed a run of four wins and two draws in their next seven games, suggesting that they could become promotion material. The 1–0 Friday night victory against Chelsea, courtesy of a Chico Hamilton penalty on 3 December, only flattered to deceive, however. Following a creditable goalless draw at Plymouth on 10 December, the Blades went into decline in their next eight League games, winning just once and losing five times. From promotion contenders, the Blades were suddenly looking like relegation material at the end of February. Clearly, Jimmy Sirrel still had a massive job on his hands to bring success back to Bramall Lane.

Sheffield United 2–0 Nottingham Forest Division Two

19 March 1977

Since their 2–1 home victory over Oldham on 27 December, United had gone seven League games without a win and had been knocked out of the FA Cup at Newcastle following a third-round replay. Finally, on Tuesday 8 March the Blades secured both points at home to Cardiff with an impressive 3–0 victory. That week marked the closing of the transfer window and, with Blades fans looking for significant signings to ease what, by now, were serious relegation worries, there was hope that manager Jimmy Sirrel and chairman John Hassall would deliver them. The only activity at the Lane, however, involved turning down a five-figure bid for midfielder John Speight, who was just returning from injury but had not played since the end of October, and the signing of right-back John Cutbush, initially on loan from Fulham, with the deal later extended to a permanent £10,000 signing. This was not what the fans had expected and, given the dissatisfaction with the team's form, rumours began to circulate that there would be changes at the top – manager or chairman, or maybe even both. One particular gripe of many Unitedites was an obsession over finances and a determination not to accept the realities of the truly awful situation that the club was in. It was suggested in some quarters that there was plenty of money to spend, that the club were still sitting on the transfer money they had received from the sale of Tony Currie before the start of the season.

Chairman John Hassall chose a meeting of development fund agents in Rotherham on 15 March to reiterate the severe financial problems that United were experiencing and to offer his full support to Jimmy Sirrel. The manager was also present to express his thanks for the key work that the agents were doing to help the club's financial situation. Hassall declared that it had been impossible to make signings of top players before the transfer deadline 'due to our present financial dilemma', and that 'developing a first-class youth policy' would ultimately help the playing squad to improve. Yet patience would be required and 'given time, Jimmy Sirrel will do the job for us.' Sirrel, Hassal reminded everyone, had taken Notts County from the verge of extinction to the top of the Second Division. The chairman was, therefore, solidly behind him, 'I'm prepared to back his judgement to the limit.'

The Blades were going into the Forest game having lost narrowly at Burnley 1–0 in their previous fixture on 12 March. The bad news for Sirrel was that he would be without centre-forward Chris Guthrie, substituted at Turf Moor and still suffering from a leg strain. The manager made three changes to his team selection: defender Steve Faulkner and midfielders Steve Ludlam and Chico Hamilton were out, in came John Cutbush at right-back, Dennis Longhorn in midfield and Simon Stainrod up front. On 26 points from 29 games, the Blades were only four points above third-from-bottom Fulham. A win was vital if the Blades were to keep clear of the relegation places and, having lost 6–1 at the City Ground back in October, the players knew that they were in for a tough afternoon.

Forest, under the irrepressible management duo of Brian Clough and Peter Taylor, also needed to win, but for the opposite reason to United. In the hunt for promotion all season, Forest had experienced a poor run of late and had slipped to the fringes of the promotion pack. With 34 points from 29 games, Forest were in seventh place. With three clubs automatically promoted, Forest were seven points behind leaders Chelsea – although they had two games in hand – and were five points behind third-placed Bolton, having played the same number of games. Needing to kick-start Forest's promotion push, Clough was treating the game like a Cup tie. Forest's routine was changed: on Friday, training took place in the afternoon, not the morning, and then the team made the short journey to Sheffield and stayed in a hotel overnight. Clough had brought a strong squad with him, many of whom would be key members of the Forest side that would be champions of the First Division the following season: Viv Anderson, Frank Clark, John McGovern, Ian Bowyer, Gary Birtles, Martin O'Neill, Peter Withe, Tony Woodcock and John Robertson. Most would also feature in Forest's later European Cup triumphs.

The importance of the game to the visitors was reflected by estimates that up to 5,000 of their fans would be travelling to the game. This information created a sense of concern for the police and ground staff at Bramall Lane, in an age where football hooliganism was a significant problem and the said authorities had not yet developed effective strategies to counter it. At Bramall Lane, as at other grounds at this time, there was no real segregation policy, and as such it was extremely difficult to guarantee against violent confrontations between opposing fans inside football grounds. In addition, there was no real network of intelligence gathering in relation to identifying potential hooligans. Visiting fans were encouraged – and expected – to stand at the Bramall Lane end, but many Unitedites also chose to stand there. Most such United fans were not looking to cause trouble, but increasingly certain young fans had started to go there – and away supporters into the Shoreham Street Kop – who were looking for a confrontation. The club had appealed to home fans not to go to the Bramall Lane end, or alternatively to the corner of the John Street Terrace and Bramall Lane to chant at the visiting fans. 'Join your pals on the Kop' was a rather naive appeal though, given the gang mentality of the yobs.

Most worrying for Sheffied secretary Keith Walker was that both sets of fans would be decked out in red and so potentially difficult to set apart. As a result, Walker and the club decided to get tough, declaring, 'Any United fans going on to the Bramall Lane end tomorrow will be assumed to have gone there looking for trouble' and would be ejected by the police, arrested and prosecuted. Fortunately no major incidents were reported at the game.

Sheffield United: Brown, Cutbush, Garner, Franks, Colquhoun, Kenworthy, Woodward, Longhorn, Edwards, Hamson, Stainrod. Substitute: Hamilton
Nottingham Forest: Middleton, Anderson, Clark, Chapman, Lloyd, Bowyer, McGovern, O'Neill, Withe, Woodcock, Robertson. Substitute: O'Hare
Referee: Mr K. McNally
Attendance: 20,370

Forest started with purpose, full of neat passing and clever approach play. As such, the Blades found themselves early on the back foot with Alan Woodward, in particular, playing in a rather withdrawn role to counter the visitors' advantage in both experience and ability. Yet for all their possession, the visitors created few clear openings in the first quarter of an hour, and with youngsters Simon Stainrod and Keith Edwards foraging around up front and Gary Hamson impressing in midfield, United also threatened. The first real chance, however, did fall to the visitors as, after 18 minutes, Colquhoun was caught in possession and Tony Woodcock pounced to fire in a goal-bound shot from which United's 'keeper, Jim Brown, made a brilliant reflex save.

The Blades' response was a glancing header from Colquhoun that was blocked by a defender, before John Robertson, with space in the United area, scooped the ball over the bar. This was the signal for a period of Forest dominance in which it seemed certain that they would break the deadlock. With Chapman and Lloyd in command at the back and

Alan Woodward chips the ball over the Nottingham Forest wall from a free-kick. The first man to break after it...Keith Edwards, of course.

their midfield orchestrating some fine attacking moves, Forest were seriously threatening Brown's goal. John Robertson, tricky and dangerous, was starting to open up the right flank of United's defence, the Scot firing in a shot that went narrowly wide. Yet the Blades were fighting hard, sticking to their task and determined to hold their opponents at bay. After 37 minutes the team's commitment was rewarded when they went ahead. A foul by Chapman on the edge of the Forest area brought the Blades a free-kick. Dennis Longhorn chipped the ball into the area, where Eddie Colquhoun lifted it across goal and Keith Edwards placed a low diving header past 'keeper John Middleton to put the Blades a goal up.

Forest had every reason to feel that their play had not warranted them going behind, but young Keith Edwards had shown them the importance of having a final product at the end of their intricate footballing moves. Trying to draw level, Tony Woodcock went on a good run, only to be denied by Tony Kenworthy's timely and decisive tackle. On the verge of half-time it was United who almost scored again. Simon Stainrod made an excellent break down the right but, failing to get his head up, did not notice Colin Franks unmarked on his left and ultimately lost possession of the ball to the retreating Forest defence.

The second half began with much the same pattern as the first: Forest having most of the possession and producing some fine approach play, but without unduly troubling Jim Brown. There was danger after 55 minutes as a long clearance allowed Woodcock to race through, but Brown was quickly off his line, rushing the Forest man into a left-foot shot that just cleared the crossbar. Forest followed up with a shot by Peter Withe that flashed just wide. At the other end, a ball into the area by Alan Woodward saw Middleton just hold onto the ball as he raced out to deny the onrushing Edwards.

After 68 minutes the match experienced its moment of real controversy. A clearance over the top was raced onto by Edwards and Stainrod who, with the linesman's flag kept

Simon Stainrod takes on Frank Clark in the 2–1 victory over Forest. The camera also catches a thoughtful Jimmy Sirrel in the background.

firmly down, had beaten Forest's offside trap and were in the clear. Edwards, ahead of Simon Stainrod, lifted the ball over the advancing Middleton, only to see the ball come back off the crossbar. Stainrod, however, had continued his run and knocked the ball into the empty net. With the linesman's flag continuing to stay down, United – and their fans – were celebrating the goal, only for referee Mr McNally to disallow it for offside: the only man in the ground who seemingly did not see that Stainrod had run from behind Edwards! Dismissing United's protests, Mr McNally incensed the home players and supporters even further when, just a minute later, Brown diving at the feet of Woodcock – who appeared offside – seemed to have been fouled. When Eddie Colquhoun confronted the referee about his failure to award a free-kick, he almost inevitably found his way into the notebook!

With 12 minutes to go Woodcock was replaced by John O'Hare as Forest went all out for the equaliser. United's players, clearly feeling the injustice of Stainrod's disallowed goal, bravely and with all credit, stuck to their task. With Forest's attacks continuing to lack the killer instinct, it was young Edwards who, in injury time, showed them how it was done. Dennis Longhorn won the ball, sent it forward and Keith Edwards, latching onto it, advanced and struck a shot past Middleton and in off the post to seal a 2–0 victory.

It was a morale-boosting win for the Blades and built on the splendid performances of

United's youngsters: 19-year-old Keith Edwards, 18-year-old Tony Kenworthy and Simon Stainrod and 17-year-old Gary Hamson. Hamson's performance was made even more impressive by the fact that he was rushed to hospital straight after the match for X-rays, which showed that he had broken a bone in his hand. Impressively, the injury did not stop him playing in the following game. For Keith Edwards the game was also significant as it marked the start of a scoring run that saw him hit the net in eight successive games, a post-war United goalscoring record for the promising young striker.

The Forest fixture was followed by three away games in which the Blades struggled to get a single point. A run of four wins in their next five matches, however, saw them end the season safely in mid-table. As for Forest, the defeat galvanised them. Winning eight and drawing two of their last 12 games, they sneaked into the final promotion place by a single point from Bolton and Blackpool. Few at Bramall Lane would have dared to predict that, following their defeat by the relegation-threatened Blades, within three years Forest would be champions of England once and Europe twice!

Match 24

Cardiff City 1–6 Sheffield United
Division Two

3 December 1977

U nited had made a disastrous start to the new season. Having won just one and losing five of their first seven League fixtures, the club had parted company with manager Jimmy Sirrel on 27 September. Chief coach Cec Coldwell took over as caretaker manager, while John Hassall and the United board took their time to find the right successor to Sirrel. Restoring confidence in the players and creating a happier atmosphere in the changing room, Coldwell tightened up the defence and inspired key senior players to regain their form and appetite for the game. Starting with a 3–2 home win over one of the promotion favourites Southampton on 1 October, the re-energised Blades team went on a run of eight games undefeated, which included five successive home wins and three away draws. The unbeaten run ended with a three-goal

United's caretaker manager Cec Coldwell.

defeat at Charlton on 19 November and the following Saturday, prior to the Cardiff fixture, United were held to a 1–1 draw against Bristol Rovers at Bramall Lane.

As yet, Coldwell's team had not secured an away victory, and the acting boss targeted the Cardiff fixture as the place to get it. Coldwell told the *Sheffield Telegraph*, prior to the team travelling down to South Wales, 'If we are going to do anything at all this season we have got to win away. That provides a breathing space and gives us an extra edge.'

Significantly, Coldwell was not about to allow the team to rest on its laurels. Although 'things have been going reasonably well for the last couple of months, we have let the fans down on one or two occasions.' Coldwell was hopeful that 'we can put that right this week'.

With a full squad to pick from – Eddie Colquhoun having recovered from injury – Coldwell made just one change to the United line up. Keith Edwards, still the club's top scorer despite an eight-match lean spell, was rested in favour of fellow youngster Simon Stainrod, who was playing his first game of the season. Coldwell noted that Edwards hadn't been 'lively, sharp or buzzing in the last few games'. A young man, still learning his trade, Edwards was suffering from a lack of form and confidence, usual in the development of such players. Coldwell had spoken to Keith, telling him 'that it was in his own interests to have a spell in the reserves to get back his confidence and timing.' This is just what Stainrod had done, impressing in the reserves' victory at Newcastle previous week and, according to Coldwell, 'he deserves a go.'

Cardiff City: Irwin, Attley, Pethard, A. Campbell, Went, Thomas, Giles, Dwyer, Sayer, Robson, Buchanan. Substitute: Bishop

Sheffield United: Brown, Cutbush, Calvert, Kenworthy, Colquhoun, Flynn, Woodward, Stainrod, B. Campbell, Hamson, Hamilton. Substitute: Franks

Referee: Mr A. Hamil

Attendance: 6,395

Six coachloads of United fans had made their way down to Ninian Park for the early 2.15pm start and probably wished they had not bothered, as Cardiff came out all guns blazing in the game's opening exchanges. Two early chances for United's Bobby Campbell were soon forgotten as the Bluebirds took control of midfield and began to create a number of chances. A good move between Sayer, Dwyer and Robson opened up the United defence, Keith Robson's resulting shot zipping just past the post with United 'keeper Jim Brown successfully beaten. After 12 minutes the Blades had another lucky escape. Thomas, out on the right, sent in a cross, which Robson headed against the inside of the post. The ball bounced back along the goalline and into the relieved Jim Brown's hands. The Cardiff player was adamant that the ball had crossed the line, but the linesmen disagreed and referee Mr Hamil waved play on. The near miss encouraged

Cardiff to take an even stronger grip on the game and United found it hard to get forward, especially as Alan Woodward was having to drop deeper to help out his defence. It seemed only a question of time before the home side scored as they forced a succession of corners; a vital Bobby Campbell header crucially keeping the ball out of United's net. Peter Sayer was particularly prominent in Cardiff's attacks, and only a smart save by Jim Brown kept out the young international's shot.

After 26 minutes, however, the whole complexion of the match changed. Chico Hamilton broke down the United right on a rare foray into Cardiff territory. Hamilton passed the ball inside to Cliff Calvert, up in support, and the full-back ran on and smashed a fierce shot from 20 yards that 'keeper Bill Irwin allowed to slip through his hands and into the net to put the Blades in front. The goal proved to be, in the words of Trevor Scrafton of the *Telegraph*, 'The end of Cardiff City Football Club as far as the day's proceedings were concerned. They died a lingering and ignominious death.'

Straight away Bobby Campbell almost made it 2–0 as he burst through the Cardiff defence, but when Bill Irwin came out he rushed his chip, which went wide of the mark. United's tough young striker did not have long to wait to get on the score sheet, however. After 34 minutes Alan Woodward took a free-kick from midway inside the Cardiff half. The ball was floated over the defence and Bobby Campbell, running in from the left and unmarked, put a firm, low header into the net. A training ground set play routine, Woodward and Campbell had worked the move to perfection. With the Blades continuing to attack, two minutes before half-time they were three goals to the good. Again it was another effective set piece as, following Chico Hamilton's right-wing corner, Bobby Campbell fiercely headed home.

Cardiff, leaving the pitch to a chorus of boos from their own supporters, expected and received a half-time dressing down. United, although three goals up, received the same, Cec Coldwell explaining, 'I didn't think we played particularly well in the first half.' Until Calvert's goal had gone in, Coldwell was right and he now wanted his team on their guard as Cardiff prepared to launch the inevitable onslaught to get back into the game.

For a few minutes of the second period Coldwell was right. City threatened and Jim Brown was called on to produce a brilliant save as John Buchanan hit a fierce close-range right-footed shot that the 'keeper parried and then smothered, with Cardiff boots flying in to apply the final touch. Throwing men forward, Cardiff were almost caught on the break after 50 minutes as Bobby Campbell broke down the right, and his ball into Simon Stainrod in the Cardiff area was blocked by a last-ditch interception. Yet Cardiff's relief was short-lived as, two minutes later, Tony Kenworthy smashed home an unstoppable 20-yard shot, seizing on a loose ball created by Campbell and Stainrod's unsettling of the home defence. Four minutes later – Cardiff now having totally collapsed – a free-kick was awarded to United on the edge of the area. Alan Woodward touched the ball off to Chico Hamilton, who blasted it straight past Irwin to make it 5–0.

The Blades were not finished and continued their search for more goals. Five minutes from time Alan Woodward, on 149 League goals, seized on a loose ball in midfield, advanced, looked up and hit a thunderbolt from 25 yards that thumped against the crossbar with Irwin rooted to the spot. 'Woody' was not to be denied, however, and two minutes from time Simon Stainrod opened up the home defence and fed the ball to Alan Woodward, who slotted the ball inside the 'keeper's left-hand post to make it 6–0.

In the final minute Cardiff managed to score themselves, as John Buchanan put the ball in the net as the referee blew for time. Most of the Cardiff fans present, who had not headed for the exits in light of their team's drubbing, believed that the strike had come too late and roundly booed Mr Hamil as he left the pitch. Nevertheless, the goal did stand. With a final score of 6–1, the travelling Blades were in ecstasy, and Cardiff's consolton goal was unable to take the gloss off United's first away victory of the season.

Champagne celebrations were the order of the day as United's staff and players celebrated Alan Woodward's landmark 150th League goal. But manager Cec Coldwell was not fooled by the margin of victory and was keeping his own, and the players', feet firmly on the ground. Nevertheless, in 26 years at Bramall Lane, Cec could not remember the last time a United side had scored so many goals in an away League fixture, and he was absolutely delighted. Yet, he noted, 'We didn't play as well today as we did at Charlton a fortnight ago and we lost there 3–0. But that's football.' The local media tended to agree. The Blades had been poor in the first 25 minutes and, after that, Cardiff were too ready to roll over. What had made a real difference, though, was United's finishing. *The Star's* Tony Pritchett referred to 'United's clinical destruction of a wilting, surrendering Cardiff side', while Trevor Scrafton of the *Telegraph* flamboyantly wrote 'Coldwell's red army did a monumental destruction job on the poor, dumbfounded Welshmen, with finishing so cold-bloodedly ruthless that Johann Cruyff for his Dutch masters would have been proud of it.'

With United now playing so well and having moved up to eighth position in the League table, speculation increased that perhaps, after all, Cec Coldwell, as caretaker manager, should have his role made permanent. As yet, however, there were no signs of any resolution to the managerial issue from chairman John Hassall and the Bramall Lane board.

Match 25

Sheffield United 2–2 Tottenham Hotspur Division Two

2 January 1978

United followed up their victory over Cardiff with a 2–0 home win over high-flying Blackburn the following week. Inconsistency then began to creep into the performances in the period leading up to the Spurs game, the Blades winning two and losing two of their next four games. The two defeats – 3–0 at Oldham and 4–0 at Luton – were quite heavy, and United had both Bobby Campbell and John Flynn sent off when three down at Boundary Park. The Blades did perform well when winning 3–2 at Hull City on New Year's Eve, given that the Tigers were fighting fiercely against relegation. That performance had, therefore, given the team optimism going into what would be a tough game against promotion-contenders Tottenham Hotspur.

Tottenham had been relegated, bottom of the First Division, at the end of the 1976–77 season. There had been much pessimism prior to the opening of the new campaign at White Hart Lane, but Spurs had started well under Barnsley-born manager Keith Burkinshaw and were strong promotion contenders by the end of December. Together with Bolton, Spurs were considered to be the strongest side in the division, and they had built a reputation as an excellent passing side based around a powerful midfield that included Neil McNab, Glenn Hoddle, Steve Perryman and John Pratt. Peter Taylor – a £200,000 signing from Crystal Palace and full England international – provided danger down the flanks, and Colin Lee and John Duncan were dangerous strikers in the division. Having been beaten 4–2 by Spurs back on the opening day of the season, the Blades knew that they were facing a dangerous attacking side.

Interestingly, United had signed young Spurs defender Andy Keeley on 30 December on a free transfer. The young prospect did not find his way into the first team for a couple of weeks, however, acclimatising to his new club in the reserves. The Hull City game had seen two goals from youngster Simon Stainrod and another from Keith Edwards who, having been rested by Coldwell, was restored to the side, recharged and back to his lively and alert self. Edwards had been brought back to replace the suspended Bobby Campbell, who was serving a three-match ban for violent conduct.

Sheffield United: Brown, Cutbush, Calvert, Kenworthy, Colquhoun, Flynn, Woodward, Edwards, Stainrod, Longhorn, Hamilton. Substitute: Hamson, replacing Flynn
Tottenham Hotspur: Daines, Naylor, Holmes, Hoddle, McAlister, Perryman, Pratt, McNab, Duncan, Lee, Taylor. Substitute: Armstrong
Referee: Mr A. McDonald
Attendance: 31,207

The attendance of over 30,000 brought in record receipts for United, the holiday crowd eager to see how the Blades coped with the challenge of Spurs. The size of the task became immediately apparent as the visitors began to put together some slick and incisive passing moves that had the United defence in real trouble. Eddie Colquhoun received a harsh booking for dissent, following a first-minute foul on Colin Lee, which certainly did not help the United defence to settle. After six minutes, with the visitors well on top, Blades 'keeper Jim Brown made a superb save from Peter Taylor to keep the game level. Other chances continued to come for Spurs: Duncan headed over a good opportunity and McNab, storming through into the box, was denied by a superbly-timed tackle by John Flynn. It was not until around the half-hour mark that United finally began to gain the confidence to take the game to their opponents. It seemed that there was too much admiration for the quality being exhibited by the visitors, which, although impressive, lacked a real end product. Nevertheless, despite the odd half-chance falling to strikers Simon Stainrod and Keith Edwards, there was little to trouble Spurs goalkeeper Barry Daines in the opening half. Not so Jim Brown, who again pulled off a superb save, this time from Neil McNab, just before half-time.

United were lucky to be level at the break, having been effectively outplayed for most of the first half. Emerging for the second period, the Blades players finally began to show the belief that they could take something from the game and started to exert pressure on the Spurs defence. After 53 minutes Daines made a super save from a shot by Alan Woodward, and as the ball broke loose it was quickly cleared to McNab, who played a precision ball through United's defence for left-back Jimmy Holmes, charging through, to beat the offside trap. Holmes, advancing on the exposed Jim Brown, squared the ball to John Duncan, in support, who miskicked the ball in front of the open net, almost allowing Jim Brown to recover and scoop the ball out. Unfortunately, Brown's reach exceeded his grasp and the ball trickled over the line to make it 1–0 to the visitors.

It was ironic that Spurs, unable to score in a first half that they had totally dominated, had gone ahead in a period of United pressure. Worse was to come, as within a minute the visitors were two goals up. Glenn Hoddle made progress down the right and played the ball across to Peter Taylor on the left, who fired the ball past Brown. As *The Star's* Tony Pritchett noted, 'Few people in the ground doubted then that it was all over.' Yet the goal simply resurrected United's desire, belief and character; collectively the players rose to the challenge and were determined to get back into the game, taking the match to Spurs in a wave of attacks. The Blades got their reward after 65 minutes. Cliff Calvert robbed the ball from Glen Hoddle in midfield and surged down the United left. Spotting Ian Hamilton, Calvert passed him the ball and then 'Chico' whipped over a fine cross into the centre, where Keith Edwards, peeling off his covering defender at the far post, planted an accurate downward header past Daines to make it 2–1.

Immediately, Coldwell pulled off the injured John Flynn for young midfielder Gary Hamson. The initiative stayed with United, but Daines was looking solid, like Brown, in goal. With 10 minutes to go, however, he was finally undone. As Simon Stainrod went on a run to the edge of the area, he was surrounded by Spurs defenders. Firing the ball in, it rebounded off an opponent – a hand, claimed Stainrod and other United forwards – and, in the confusion, Gary Hamson ignored everything and struck the ball into the bottom right-hand corner, the unsighted Daines actually falling to the left. As the ball hit the back of the net at the Shoreham Street End, the Kop went wild with delight. It was a tremendous comeback and the match could yet be won.

With a cauldron of noise behind them and chants of 'Bring on the Arsenal' – United's FA Cup visitors on the coming Saturday – ringing around the ground, the Blades went for the jugular. Woodward almost scored as he headed narrowly wide of the post and Edwards slipped the Spurs offside trap but was denied by Daines. The visitors were probably relieved when they heard the final whistle, but given their dominant first-half display, the result was probably fair. Both managers were full of praise for both sets of players and the quality of the entertainment that had been served up for the fans.

Again Cec Coldwell's team had shown itself to be one of real character and ability. They had recovered against arguably the best side in the division and the local reporters were optimistic about what the rest of the season could bring. Peter Ferguson at the *Telegraph* noted that 'Sheffield United's 1978 should be one to savour if they can reproduce performances like this one that rattled mighty Tottenham.' Tony Pritchett, meanwhile, posed an interesting suggestion: 'Coldwell must be satisfied with the general commitment of his team. The introduction of a couple more quality players – if they could be found – would make life very interesting indeed at Bramall Lane in the New Year.'

For all Cec Coldwell's good work, however, it was clear that United's board wanted an experienced, proven manager to move the club forward. On 3 January, the day after the Spurs game, *The Star* made it clear that Luton's Harry Haslam was United's target – the 58-year-old manager also being sought to become Millwall's new boss and Manchester United's new chief scout. After some intricate negotiations, Haslam finally joined the Blades on 26 January, together with the Uruguayan Danny Bergara as his number two.

Meanwhile, the fans' euphoria over the performance against Tottenham was quickly knocked back as United, with another bumper crowd of 32,156 and new record receipts, were thrashed 5–0 by Arsenal – four goals down after just quarter of an hour – and then proceeded to concede five goals in each of their next two League games, against high-flying Bolton and Sunderland in the League. The latter defeats ended any realistic hopes that the Blades could force themselves into the promotion race, especially with Haslam declaring that he needed time to assess and then rebuild the playing squad. A mid-table finish was probably the best that United could hope for, and this was ultimately what was achieved. It must be remembered, however, that Coldwell's four months in charge had removed United from the dangers of relegation that were facing them at the time of Jimmy Sirrel's departure, and for this he must be given a great deal of credit.

Sheffield United 1–0 Liverpool
League Cup second round

28 August 1978

Optimistic that his team would fare well in his first full season as Blades manager, Harry Haslam was reasonably pleased with their progress in the first three League fixtures prior to the League Cup second-round tie against European champions Liverpool. United had played well in the first half of the opening game against Orient at Bramall Lane on 19 August, taking the lead early. In fact, new signing Alex Sabella's first real contribution was to take the corner that was headed in by Simon Stainrod. A sloppy second-half performance had, however, brought an Orient recovery and a 2–1 defeat for the Blades. Haslam had criticised the team's naivety and lack of concentration, and the players had responded with two good away performances. New signing John Matthews, a centre-half who cost £80,000 from Arsenal, made his debut in a 1–0 victory at Leicester on 23 August, scoring the winning goal. United followed this up with an impressive performance at Preston on 26 August, a notable game as it saw Argentinian Alex Sabella's first goal for the club, Stainrod scoring the other in a 2–2 draw.

Sabella's performances had been excellent and he certainly seemed to have breathed new life into United's rebuilt side. His transfer to the Blades from River Plate Club, at a time when foreign players, particularly South Americans, were virtually unknown in the English game, was creating huge media interest and, for now, Sabella was meeting all expectations. *The Star's* Tony Pritchett, however, noted that now the real test would come, 'after pulverising

Talented young midfielder Gary Hamson.

Leicester and Preston in two magical displays in the last few days, the man from Argentina now goes in against the best organised, most successful side in Europe.'

Manager Haslam had no qualms about Sabella's prospects of success. 'Happy Harry' enthused profusely about Sabella, saying 'he's going to be one of the greatest. There is nowhere in England I could buy a player like this for £160,000.'

Yet Haslam, an extrovert character and great media publicist for the Blades, was no fool; he realised the magnitude of the task facing United. Liverpool had completed three successive First Division wins against Queen's Park Rangers, Ipswich Town and Manchester City. The latter game had been screened on the previous Saturday's *Match of the Day* and City had been totally destroyed 4–1 at Maine Road by their Merseyside opponents. Adopting the role of underdogs, Haslam told the media, 'No one in Great Britain gives my lads a chance tonight and that suits me. All I know is that my team wants to play and, from the crowds outside the ticket office, everybody in Sheffield wants to see them play. I am not shouting about beating Liverpool, but we welcome the chance to tackle the best.'

And United would have to tackle the best. This was an era when 'squad rotation' was not in the football management vocabulary. Regardless of the competition, all teams put out their strongest side and the Blades players would indeed face the European champions. Liverpool, with no injury worries, were at full strength, and were unchanged from their first three games. The Blades were not quite so lucky. Tony Kenworthy had damaged a knee against Preston at Deepdale and had to give way for Andy Keeley, who would partner John Matthews in the centre of defence. Fortunately, left-back Paul Garner and Alex Sabella, who had also picked up knocks, were declared fit.

With the huge interest in Sheffield for the Monday night game, the club was hoping for record receipts to beat those taken from the previous season's FA Cup tie against Arsenal, where United earned £43,000 from a crowd of 32,156. With 35,753 actually attending the Liverpool game, the club were delighted to find that they had taken over £10,000 extra at the gate. The interest caused by the Sabella signing seemed to be paying off. The gamble United had taken in stretching their finances to seal the Sabella deal could, therefore, if the team continued to perform well, prove to be successful.

Sheffield United: Conroy, Cutbush, Garner, Keeley, Matthews, Speight, Woodward, Stainrod, Finnieston, Hamson, Sabella. Substitute: Franks
Liverpool: Clemence, Neal, A. Kennedy, Thompson, R. Kennedy, Hughes, Dalglish, Case, Heighway, McDermott, Souness. Substitute: Fairclough
Referee: Mr D. Lloyd
Attendance: 35,753

The quality of the opposition that United were facing was clear from the start, as Liverpool took an almost immediate grip on the game and showed that they were loathe to allow United's little Argentinian the opportunity to put in another impressive performance against them. Early on, Sabella, after brilliantly beating Kenny Dalglish, was brought down by Britain's most expensive forward. For the rest of the game it was clear that Liverpool's tough-tackling midfielder Terry McDermott had taken on the responsibility of stopping Sabella's dangerous runs: the two players almost engaged in their own private battle as the game unfolded.

Yet Liverpool, though tough, were also showing their pure class and, through Graeme Souness and Emlyn Hughes in midfield, were playing some wonderful football as they exerted almost continual pressure on the United defence. Simon Stainrod put in a good early shot for the Blades, but the reality was that the game was being played almost entirely in United's half. Fortunately, Liverpool were producing few real chances as United's rearguard, superbly marshalled by John Matthews, fought hard to restrict their opportunities to speculative long-range shots. Nevertheless, the Blades were fortunate to escape when, after 25 minutes, Dalglish had a shot blocked and the ball fell invitingly to Jimmy Case, who was unable to find the net.

United did manage managed to produce a couple of scoring chances. The first came when Stainrod threaded a great pass through to Steve Finnieston, but as the Scot moved through on goal he was cynically chopped down by Phil Neal. As United prepared to take the free-kick, referee Lloyd surprised players and spectators alike when he drew out his card and booked four Liverpool players – Dalglish, Case, McDermott and Neal – for not moving their wall back the full 10 yards. Believing that they were at the correct distance, the Liverpool players argued vociferously, but to no avail. The incident served only to disrupt the Liverpool players' concentration, with the result that, from the free-kick, Mick Speight stole in to plant a brave diving header just wide of the post. United's second opportunity, perhaps the best of the first half, came when Hamson's cross to the near post

John Matthews, commanding at the back against Liverpool.

was almost turned in by Alan Woodward. Normal service was resumed just before the break, however, when left-back Alan Kennedy fired in a shot that United's 'keeper Stephen Conroy only kept out with difficulty.

Liverpool continued to force the pace as the second half got underway, and efforts from Ray Kennedy, Kenny Dalglish, Alan Kennedy, Jimmy Case, Emlyn Hughes and substitute David Fairclough severely tested Conroy. Matthews cleared the ball off the line from Steve Heighway and then John Cutbush repeated the feat to deny Graeme Souness. United's 'keeper was playing superbly, the *Telegraph's* Trevor Scrafton declaring, 'Conroy, having everything thrown at him, including smoke bombs, reacted heroically.' Most impressive was his wonderful save, using his legs, from Ray Kennedy's ferocious shot, which resulted from a rapid counter-attack involving Alan Kennedy and Dalglish.

The second half clearly belonged to Liverpool. Completely on top, surely it was just a matter of time before they scored. With 10 minutes to go, however, the unlikely happened. On a rare foray into the Liverpool half, the ball was played into the box, where Alex Sabella and substitute Colin Franks battled for it with Emlyn Hughes and Phil Thompson. Sabella was able to take control of the ball and, although fouled, managed to push the ball out to his left, from where Gary Hamson smashed the ball past England 'keeper Ray Clemence to send the Bramall Lane crowd into an eruption of noise and excitement.

In a desperate last 10 minutes, Liverpool continued to pile forward in search of an equaliser, but with Matthews still commanding at the back, there was no way that the Blades were going to relinquish their lead, and the team held on for a famous and memorable victory.

It had been a one-sided game, totally dominated by the European champions in every aspect, apart from the one that ultimately mattered – scoring goals. The Blades had certainly experienced a great deal of luck, but all commentators agreed that they had defended heroically and it had been a true team effort. As *The Star's* Tony Pritchett commented, 'The night belonged to the *team*. Matthews and Conroy were the men of the night; Hamson got the glory goal, but United carried no passengers.' For all that they were under pressure, the Blades kept their discipline, did not resort to foul tactics and, when the few opportunities presented themselves to take the offensive, did not simply launch the ball forward, but tried to attack in the passing style that Harry Haslam was trying to instill into the team's pattern of play.

Haslam was indeed 'Happy Harry' as a smile beamed all over his face in the crowded press room after the match. He acknowledged that his team had been 'under the cosh' and had ridden their luck, but was delighted with their total commitment. 'I am so pleased for everybody,' said Haslam, 'the club have backed me and it's great to see results coming and the people responding. Along the way we shall get frustrations, but it's coming right.' Bob Paisley, Liverpool's manager and Haslam's friend, was magnanimous in defeat when he addressed the United boss: 'Well done, that's what the game is all about. We had enough chances, but your lad in goal played well. You had maybe two chances in the second half and put one in. Say "good luck" to the lads for me.'

When the draw was announced for the third round of the Cup, United found that they would have another huge home fixture against Yorkshire rivals Leeds United, going well in the First Division. This was again given extra significance by the return of ex-Blades star Tony Currie to Bramall Lane. The game, on 10 October, attracted an even larger gate of 39,614 and there was much anticipation among United fans of the sub-plot to the game that pitched United's old favourite, 'TC', against their new star, Alex Sabella. Sadly, United's form dipped following the Liverpool victory, and against Leeds they found themselves outclassed and 2–0 down by half-time. Leeds cruised to an eventual 4–1 victory, Currie winning on points against Sabella. United's League Cup dream was over for another season.

Sheffield United 1–2 River Plate Club Friendly

30 August 1978

The friendly against River Plate came out of the events surrounding the signing of Alejandro (Alex) Sabella from the River Plate Club in Buenos Aires, Argentina, in July 1978. The midfielder's signature was secured for £160,000 after an enterprising mission to Argentina, hosts and winners of the 1978 World Cup, by manager Harry Haslam. Haslam had set up the deal at the end of an 11-day visit. He was accompanied by United's youth coach Oscar Arce, an Argentinian who had helped to negotiate the transfer through the assistance of the famous Antonio Rattin – the Argentine captain who had gained notoriety through being sent off at Wembley in the World Cup quarter-final against England in 1966. Rattin had visited Sheffield secretly on 22 June – three days before the World Cup Final between Argentina and Holland – and had agreed to become United's agent in Argentina and recommend players to them. Haslam's visit had initially promised the signatures of Osvaldo Ardiles and Ricardo Villa – two of Argentina's World Cup-winning side – but a delay in the negotiations enabled Spurs manager Keith Burkinshaw to gain knowledge of their availability, and his offer of £700,000 for both players was one United could not match. Graciously, Haslam agreed to sign the transfer forms for Ardiles and Villa on Tottenham's behalf, due to Burkinshaw's delayed arrival. A few days later Haslam announced that Sabella – who also had represented Argentina – had been signed. At 23 years of age, Sabella became United's record signing and Haslam declared himself

United boss 'Happy' Harry Haslam in jovial mood.

confident that Alex would develop into a better player than either of Spurs' big-name acquisitions. Interestingly, Haslam also seems to have been involved in unsuccessful negotiations to bring the 15-year-old Diego Maradona to Bramall Lane.

As part of the negotiations for Sabella's transfer, the River Plate Club agreed to play a fixture against the Blades as part of their European tour to Holland and Spain. This too was a huge coup for United, given that the River Plate still had several World Cup winners in its ranks: goalkeeper Ubaldo Filliol, centre-half Daniel Passarella, midfielder Norberte Alonso, winger Oscar Ortiz and striker Leopoldo Luque. Clearly, the opportunity to see these star players was an exciting one for Blades fans; not quite so exciting was the fact that, well before the game, the club announced that there would be 'special prices' for the fixture. *The Star*'s headline of 4 August 1978 did not mince its words, declaring, 'Record Prices at Lane Spectacular'. Seats in the centre South Stand would rise from £3.30 to £4, standing on the terrace from £1.40 to £2, the Kop from £1.20 to £1.50 and concession prices for juveniles and senior citizens would also be higher. Speaking on behalf of the club, Harry Haslam justified the rise on the grounds that supporters would be watching a side that exuded real class, saying 'their full squad is of international pedigree, even more star-spangled than, say, Liverpool.' Significantly, the commitments of Argentina's top clubs to play European friendlies meant that there could be no England versus Argentina fixture at Wembley and, therefore, the Lane game was the only chance to see half of the Argentinian World Cup-winning side in England. United, therefore, hoped that others – not just Blades fans – would turn up to watch them at Bramall Lane. Most important, perhaps, was Haslam's acknowledgement of the financial costs that River Plate's visits would bring for United, 'the huge outlay involved in getting the match here'. Given that River Plate travelled with an entourage of at least 50 players, officials and attendants, who would need to be put up in local hotels for the duration of their stay, and that a civic welcome and post match dinner for both teams and officials would be provided, the visit certainly was not going to be cheap. It perhaps explains why, although Haslam believed that 'England versus South America at club level has got to come. It's not enough for countries to meet every four years in the World Cup', the idea was always going to be a non-starter for Sheffield United; the club simply could not afford to play a game like this for the foreseeable future.

Club officials, hoping for 30,000 through the turnstiles, had to be satisfied with an attendance of 22,244 on the night. Given that United had received record receipts for the Liverpool game two nights earlier, it was clear that many supporters found this game, coming so soon after, difficult to finance. The situation was made worse by the fact that the Blades would again be at home on the following Saturday against Crystal Palace. Given the demands on the pockets of the fans, United's higher pricing policy for the River Plate game probably backfired.

Preparations for the match itself showed the difference between the English and Argentinian training methods at that time. While United, who had already played a tough encounter against Liverpool on Monday, were training on the morning of Wednesday night's match, River Plate were approaching the encounter very differently. *The Star's* Tony Pritchett noted that 'the South American superstars slept and siested their way to tonight's big match. Their routine was a late breakfast, a walk around, a sleep in the afternoon and then on to Bramall Lane.' It was no wonder that Alex Sabella was finding his early days in England to be something of a culture shock!

While United were without Tony Kenworthy and Steve Finnieston for the game, Haslam did make Sabella captain for the night in place of normal skipper Alan Woodward. Meanwhile, all River Plate's top stars were available and in their starting line up.

Sheffield United: Brown, Cutbush, Garner, Keeley, Matthews, Speight, Woodward, Stainrod, Guy, Hamson, Sabella. Substitutes: Franks, Benjamin, Varadi

River Plate Club: Filliol, Perfumo, Cosellos, Saporiti, Merlo, Passarella, Gonsales, Merchati, Luque, Alonso, Ortiz. Substitutes: Labruna, Commisso, Bargas

Referee: Mr C. Thomas

Attendance: 22,244

For the supporters who attended, the match was an occasion to be savoured rather than a 'must win' competitive fixture. Straight from the start, the football on offer was of the highest quality. With England manager Ron Greenwood and other top football personalities in attendance, it was actually the Blades who were first to impress. Woodward and Sabella were proving particularly difficult for the River Plate defence to handle. 'Woody' forced 'keeper Filliol into some early saves with some trademark sharp shooting, while Sabella was dancing his way around his former teammates, with Saporiti given a particularly torrid time. After nine minutes Alex Sabella, in possession of the ball, rounded Merlo, advanced into the box and was just about to pull the trigger, only to be brought crashing to the ground by Saporiti. Referee Clive Thomas had no hesitation in pointing to the spot, although Ubaldo Filliol, Argentina's World Cup-winning goalkeeper, hotly disputed the award and so ended up in the referee's notebook for time-wasting and

FILLIOL   ORTIZ   PASSARELLA

Three of River Plate's World Cup winners.

arguing. Calm and composed while Filliol's histrionics were being played out, the ever-reliable Alan Woodward placed the ball on the spot, waited for the whistle and, once it came, sent Filliol the wrong way, planting the ball in the corner of the net to put the Blades ahead.

As the game developed, the Blades continued to play some fine passing football, with Sabella and Woodward ably assisted by an impressive performance from Gary Hamson in midfield. At the back, John Matthews was resolutely holding United's rearguard together, as the visitors began to get into their stride and show the silky skills that had brought the crowning of their nation as world champions. At the heart of River Plates offensive threat was Oscar Ortiz, the visitors' captain, World Cup winner and superb winger. Exhibiting magnificent ball control, passing and shooting ability and excellent thought and movement, it was always likely to be Ortiz who would bring the visitors back into the game. Before half-time Ortiz did just that as he unleashed a wicked 25-yard swerving shot that had United's 'keeper Jim Brown beaten. For the rest of the half it was a case of Alonso and Sabella displaying their brilliant skills to an enthralled and appreciative crowd, each trying to conjure up the breakthrough that would give their side the advantage. Sabella's impressive performance was certainly taking the attention of the opposition, who, although previously his colleagues, were not slow to dish out some rather heavy punishments to him. River Plate had seemingly forgotten that the match was a friendly!

At half-time the Blades were level and the crowd responded to both teams' efforts with a great ovation as the players left the pitch. Probably tired from his exertions against Liverpool, Sabella, who had matched the skill of any on the River Plate side in the opening half, was less prominent after the break. Given that the game was a friendly, Haslam was keen to give other players a taste of the action and made three changes, as did the visitors. Yet both teams continued to provide an exciting and enterprising game. Ultimately, River Plate's superior skill and magical qualities began to dominate. When, after 60 minutes, World Cup hero Leopoldo Luque smashed in a shot that, being deflected, looped over the unfortunate Brown, the visitors had the lead and never looked like surrendering it. When Passarella and Luque went off five minutes later they received a tremendous ovation from the Bramall Lane crowd: an ovation repeated for the whole River Plate team and for United's sterling efforts against them at the final whistle.

It had been a splendid match, a real vindication of the decision to bring the Argentinians to Bramall Lane. 'River Plate won with flair of confidence,' reported *The Star's* Tony Pritchett, 'but United, fast putting together an interesting football team, played their part.' At the after-match dinner at the Cutler's Hall, FA chairman Sir Harold Thompson chose the occasion to extol the virtues of Alan Woodward, declaring, 'If I had been the manager of the England team over the years and even today, I would find it difficult to overlook Alan Woodward.' It was, therefore, ironic that he was to play just one further competitive fixture for the Blades, against Crystal Palace on Saturday at the Lane, before departing for Tulsa Roughnecks and the North American Soccer League.

Following their recent victory over the European champions and narrow defeat to the champions of South America, United seemed on the verge of a successful season. Sadly, fans and local media alike were quickly brought back to earth as the Blades lost three out of four of their following League games. From the euphoria of those three days in late August, a season of nightmare proportions was about to unfold. And as for the South American connection? Antonio Rattin, United's man in Argentina, uncovered no further South American players for the Blades. In addition, the much-talked about reciprocal visit of the Blades to play River Plate in Buenos Aires at the end of the season never materialised. By that time, however, United and their fans had far more critical considerations to concern themselves with.

Match 28

Sheffield United 3–2 Sunderland Division Two

7 October 1978

United's poor run of form prior to the Sunderland fixture, with a draw and three defeats after the Liverpool and River Plate fixtures, had manager Harry Haslam in the mood to ring the changes in terms of his team selection. A week earlier United had only managed a 1–1 draw against Haslam's previous club Luton Town at Bramall Lane and Haslam had been very disappointed. The Blades' goal had been scored by Peter Anderson, who had been making his full League debut after being signed in September from Tampa Bay Rowdies, along with goalkeeper Nicky Johns. Anderson was an attacking right-sided player who had made his name under Haslam at Luton. His addition, it was hoped, would provide skill and penetration for the United attack. To assist Anderson, star-signing Alex Sabella was returning to the team following his absence against Luton, and Steve Finnieston also returned to the line up following his lengthy absence since being injured in the Liverpool game. With Nicky Johns making his League debut in goal, coming in to replace Steve Conroy, the side has been changed significantly. The most striking part of Haslam's shake up was his decision to call up 18-year-old Richard Harwood for his League debut. Harwood would play in midfield in place of Andy Keeley. Explaining his decision, Haslam declared, 'I watched Richard in midweek and it set me thinking. I watched him again, decided to rest Andy, and now it's up to the lad, and to the other players to help him along.' Finally, Simon Stainrod found himself out of the matchday 12, while Colin Franks, who had been covering as an emergency centre-forward since the injury to Finnieston, was dropped to the bench. Significantly, the game brought together Haslam's five major signings of the season for the first time in the United side: Anderson, Johns, Sabella, Matthews and Finnieston. Interestingly, the Sunderland line up contained two future Blades: Joe Bolton and Wilf Rostron.

Sheffield United: Johns, Cutbush, Calvert, Kenworthy, Matthews, Speight, Anderson, Harwood, Finnieston, Sabella, Hamson. Substitute: Franks
Sunderland: Siddall, Coady, Bolton, Docherty, Clarke, Elliott, Chisholm, Rostron, Entwistle, Brown, Rowell. Substitute: Lee
Referee: Mr R. Chadwick
Attendance: 18,873

With the BBC's *Match of the Day* cameras in attendance, it was the visitors who got off to the best start, settling down to control the game after the initial early exchanges. Sunderland's first chance fell to Brown, who muscled his way past Tony Kenworthy and fired in a goal-bound shot that Nicky Johns palmed around the post. The same player was then almost through again but was denied by a fine tackle from Mick Speight, working hard to combat Sunderland's hard-tackling, well-organised and skilful midfield. For the Blades, Alex Sabella was beginning to exhibit flashes of his South American flair, weaving through a series of tackles on a couple of occasions but as yet unable to deliver the decisive pass needed to unlock the disciplined Sunderland defence. Nevertheless, Sabella, brought down on the edge of the Sunderland area, gained United a free-kick that, taken by John Matthews, brought a fine save from the visitors' 'keeper Barry Siddall.

Just before the half-hour Nicky Johns, who had shown signs of nervousness and who had been ineffective in his kicking and clearances, lost possession of a cross and it seemed that Sunderland would score. Fortunately for the Blades, referee Chadwick ruled that Johns had been unfairly pushed by Wayne Entwistle. United's response to the scare was another fine run by Sabella, who was again fouled. This time Gary Rowell was booked. From the resulting free-kick, young Harwood gained possession and turned the ball into the area, where Steve Finnieston connected, only for Siddall to make another good save at the foot of his post.

After 32 minutes a defensive mix-up provided Sunderland with the lead. In possession of the ball outside his own area, Tony Kenworthy was caught in two minds over whether to clear the ball himself or pass it back to 'keeper Nicky Johns. Delaying, Kenworthy knocked the ball back to Johns, who, also unduly hesitant, allowed Brown to nip in. Fighting to gain possession, the two players fell to the ground. Brown, reacting smartly, pushed the ball across the goal to Gary Rowell, who, following up, pushed the ball home

Argentinian ace Alejandro (Alex) Sebella.

to give the visitors the lead. Although Haslam later defended Johns, the Lane crowd were convinced it was the new 'keeper's fault that their team were a goal down.

It was a catastrophic goal, and United's confidence could have been severely shaken, but, to their credit, they fought back well in the period up to half-time. In particular, Gary Hamson was showing some good touches in midfield and was starting to dominate his opponents. It was Hamson who got on the end of a low cross by Cutbush to bring another smart save from Siddall, while John Matthews also fired in a fierce shot for the Blades that just went wide. Under pressure, Sunderland had two further players booked: Chisholm for a high tackle on Hamson and Joe Bolton for tripping Finnieston.

Having got themselves organised, and effective as a unit in the final minutes of the first half, the Blades went on to produce some brilliant attacking football in the second. After 57 minutes United's endeavour was rewarded with an exciting and incisive attacking move that saw Mick Speight send Gary Hamson away down the left, and his perfect low cross was swept into the Sunderland net by Peter Anderson, charging through the middle.

Yet, with Johns lacking any real certainty or command of his area, the United defence continued to look nervous and uncertain. Almost immediately after the equaliser, Tony Kenworthy again failed to clear and, in the mêlée of players in the United box, the ball broke to Wayne Entwistle, who put the ball into the net. Fortune was on United's side, however, as the flag was up for offside and the Blades were again let off the hook.

Regardless of their jitters at the back, the Blades were continuing to impress up front as Sabella, Hamson, Anderson and Finnieston were making space, linking up and creating a series of scoring opportunities. After 70 minutes it was perhaps inevitable that United went in front. Harwood began the move on the left, playing the ball out to Sabella, whose trickery got him beyond his opponents and enabled him to play a precision pass into the Sunderland area. Here, Peter Anderson, running on to the ball, showed great control to take it past Jeff Clarke one way and then hit the ball in the other direction, slotting it past the bemused Barry Siddall to put the Blades ahead 2–1. A great goal, and the Lane crowd erupted in appreciation of two great pieces of skill.

With Anderson denied a hat-trick by a brilliant save from Siddall, as the game entered its final five minutes United still needed a cushion to make the game safe. It came following another example of Sabella's genius. The Argentinian tricked and wriggled his way past a succession of defenders out on the right, drove to the goalline and then pulled a great ball back to Steve Finnieston, who, in the right place at the right time, slotted the ball home for 3–1. Disappointingly, in the final minute, the United defence again showed a lack of discipline as they were carved wide open and Bob Lee made the final score 3–2.

Given that the 'Famous Five' had appeared together for the first time, focus naturally tended to be on the positive and encouraging signs of United's second-half performance, rather than their more nervous, error-strewn first-half display. Certainly, there was much to admire after half-time and Finnieston, Anderson and Sabella seemed to have linked up very well together. The performance of Gary Hamson was also outstanding and it seemed as if the Blades, in this vein, would be a match for any of the top teams in the division. Encouraging also was the performance of young Richard Harwood. He had been forced off the field two minutes from time with cramp, but he had clearly shown that he had the ability to perform at this level and was rewarded by Haslam by keeping his place for the next two games against Leeds and Millwall. Harwood, however, was not to have a professional career of any longevity. He made just one further appearance, as a substitute against Cardiff in December, and left United to enter non-League football. Nicky Johns, nervous against Sunderland, was equally questionable in the following match against Leeds and he would be out of the team and sold on to Charlton in December for £135,000, recouping most of the money that United had laid out for him.

Following the victory over Sunderland, there was much excitement over the upcoming League Cup game against Leeds United and Tony Currie. As previously noted, the Blades were soundly beaten in the fixture, but there was still optimism that the team could climb the Second Division table and fight for promotion. With all their new signings in place and, hopefully, a settled team, this did not seem an unrealistic objective. A draw at Millwall, followed by a home win over Oldham and then an excellent performance at second-placed Stoke on 28 October, where United were very unlucky to lose, seemed to indicate that the team were well on course. But then the wheels fell off. Inexplicably, the Blades went on a run of five defeats and one draw in their next six League games. Promotion, regardless of Haslam's new players, new regimes and new playing style, was not on the agenda; now it was looking like a question of survival. The end of December seemed to offer new hope, however, as United finally won back-to-back games at Bramall Lane, against Cardiff 2–1 on 16 December and Newcastle 1–0 on Boxing Day. Hopefully, the corner had been turned.

Match 29

Sheffield United 2–1 Charlton Athletic
Division Two

28 April 1979

United's victories against Cardiff and Newcastle in December flattered to deceive. Haslam had declared himself buoyed up by the recent performances, saying 'Roll on 1979, I am looking forward to the new year tremendously.' In the following game, at home to Cambridge on 30 December, however, the Blades were leading 2–0 and Gary Hamson then missed a spot-kick, which would have made it 3–0. Cambridge then recovered to secure a 3–3 draw. This set the club on a run of 10 League games before they secured another victory against Bristol Rovers at Bramall Lane on 31 March. United had thus slipped into serious relegation trouble, although six draws had at least put points on the board and kept them in with a good chance of survival.

The period also saw the arrival of centre-half John MacPhail from Dundee for £30,000, in an attempt to strengthen the back four after Colin Franks and Cliff Calvert had been allowed to depart for Toronto Blizzards in the North American Soccer League. With Imre Varadi also being sold to Everton for £80,000, at a time when the club was clearly struggling, Haslam acknowledged in his programme notes for the Stoke City game on 10 March, 'It is quite natural that supporters should ask why at this time we dispose of players in the transfer market, particularly when I have expressed satisfaction at the way they may have played.' Yet the manager insisted that the moves were right for the club; Varadi was an undeveloped talent, and Franks and Calvert had repeatedly requested to leave for America.

The manager asked the fans to get behind the team: 'The players need encouragement. Let them know you're behind them, even when things are not going well and they will come right.' The fans certainly could not be criticised for their vociferous support on the road, as the away following, despite the problems, remained very strong.

With the transfer deadline looming at the end of March, Haslam acquired left-back Les Tibbott from Ipswich for £100,000, but, most importantly, made an inspired loan signing in securing midfielder Bruce Rioch from Derby County. Rioch was an accomplished and combative player, who had captained Scotland in the 1978 World Cup Finals in Argentina. His first two appearances saw the Blades climb out of the relegation places as successive home victories were secured against Bristol Rovers 1–0 on 31 March and West Ham United 3–0 on 2 April. In an eight-game spell with Rioch, United secured four wins and a draw, although heavy defeats in Rioch's last two games, 4–0 at Cardiff and 6–0 at Sunderland, prior to the Charlton game, left the Blades still in the bottom three. Most United fans would agree, however, that Rioch had proved a good influence on the team. For whatever reason, the chance to re-sign him was not taken, and so the Blades had to complete their crucial final four fixtures without him.

When United hosted Charlton on 28 April both teams were in serious relegation trouble. The Blades occupied the final relegation spot, with 31 points and four games left, while Charlton were two places higher, on 33 points, but with only two games to play. The Blades, therefore, had a real opportunity to overhaul their rivals.

Harry Haslam was certainly feeling the pressure prior to the game, especially after the heavy defeats at Cardiff and Sunderland. It was far from the situation early in the season when optimism was high and it was assumed that United would be serious promotion contenders. Commenting on the situation, Haslam declared, 'Sure, I feel a lot of pressure. I worry deeply about how the club is doing. Changes had to be made and obviously certain things can rebound on you.' Yet the manager remained optimistic. Playing down the Sunderland defeat, he insisted, 'We played reasonably well – it wasn't a daft performance like the one at Cardiff.' Haslam was confident that the players would put in a good performance against the Addicks.

The Blades were weakened by the loss of Rioch, who had returned to Derby and, in addition, Steve Finnieston was doubtful with a groin strain and John Matthews was still unavailable with ligament damage. Yet Haslam insisted that 'the other lads will raise themselves, they know what's at stake.' As it turned out, Finnieston was available for the game. Meanwhile, Charlton had recalled their prolific striker Derek Hales and, having earlier defeated United 3–1 at the Valley, were quietly confident. In goal, Charlton had Nicky Johns, who had played two disastrous games for the Blades back in August.

Sheffield United: Conroy, Cutbush, Tibbott, Kenworthy, Garner, Speight, Anderson, Guy, Finnieston, Sabella, Hamson.

Charlton Athletic: Johns, Shaw, Campbell, Churchouse, Berry, Madden, Powell, Gritt, Robinson, Hales, Brisley.
Attendance: 16,888

To the delight of the Blades fans, the team began with real endeavour, playing with an incisiveness that belied their recent performances. Having dominated the early exchanges, Peter Anderson opened the scoring after 24 minutes when he headed home a cross from John Cutbush. Just after half-time United had two, with Mike Guy firing past Johns from Finnieston's through ball. Other chances came United's way as Argentinian midfielder Alex Sabella and Anderson began to rediscover their form. Yet the crucial third goal, which would have secured the points, just would not come and the Blades, especially Guy and Anderson, were guilty of some glaring misses. In addition, Nicky Johns, gaining some satisfaction after his sorry time with the Blades, was playing well. His stop from a deflected Speight shot being particularly impressive.

With 15 minutes to go, disaster struck. Powell crossed into the box for an unmarked Hales to head past Conroy. The goal totally deflated the Blades, showing the fragility of their recently-won confidence. Back came the uncertainty of recent weeks: 'Passes went astray, tackles were missed and every phase of their play was characterised by a nerve-jangling lack of self-belief,' observed the *Sheffield Telegraph's* Peter Hegarty. After what seemed like an eternity, referee Donald Shaw blew the whistle and the Blades fans were jubilant. After all, United were now level with the Addicks and had two games in hand. Surely the Blades were saved.

The fans' relief and joy at the final whistle was shared by Haslam, who, regardless of his side's nervousness at the end, was full of optimism: 'We've got to win all our remaining matches,' declared United's boss in his post-match interviews, 'and I don't see why we shouldn't. I feel a lot easier now we've got back on the winning path.' With two out of their three remaining games at home, Haslam had every reason, he believed, to feel confident. Blackburn were up next at Bramall Lane and Haslam bullishly declared, 'I'm looking forward to Wednesday. The fact that Blackburn are sure to go down could make them relax a little, and when teams relax, they can leave gaps.'

Haslam's optimism was mirrored in equal measure by the pessimism of Charlton's manager Andy Nelson. The Blades were now level on points with his team and had two games in hand on the Addicks, who had just one fixture left. A realist, Nelson declared, 'We're almost certain to go down, unless we beat Oldham and other sides do very silly things.'

The 'silly thing's' referred to by Nelson were about to happen, however, and, from a position of feeling that they were almost safe, United's whole season effectively unravelled over the course of the next two games. Haslam's optimism over the Blackburn match came back to haunt him, as four days later Rovers proved tough, uncompromising opponents and, despite having a player sent off and being down to 10 men, pulled off a morale-sapping 1–0 victory at Bramall Lane. On the final Saturday of the season, 5 May, the Blades travelled to Cambridge United needing to secure at least a point to give them the opportunity to escape relegation in their rearranged home fixture against Leicester City on the following Tuesday evening. With Charlton playing, and defeating, Oldham at home, United, although cheered on by a vociferous away following, and with their destiny still in their own hands, surrendered tamely and were defeated by a goal to nil at the Abbey Stadium. Now two points behind Charlton and needing a big win to equal Charlton's points total and overhaul them on goal average, the Blades could only manage a 2–2 draw. In despair, some of United's young fans launched a misguided pitch invasion before the end – perhaps hoping to get the game abandoned and so give the Blades the chance of securing a significant victory in a replay – but it was all in vain and United were relegated. It had seemed unthinkable after the victory against Charlton, but it was a fact. United would join neighbours Wednesday in the Third Division for the first time in their illustrious history. The city that was the birthplace of modern football suffered the darkest day in its history as both of its proud and famous teams were floundering in football obscurity.

Sheffield United 1–1 Grimsby Town
Division Three

29 December 1979

After an uncertain start to their first-ever campaign in the third tier of English football, United had gone on a tremendous run of nine wins out of 10 League games, which meant that, following their 2–1 victory at Brentford on 22 October, the Blades were runaway leaders of the division and looking a safe bet for promotion. Yet uncertainty soon set in, and in the period up to Christmas inconsistent performances produced a return of just three wins and a draw out of eight League games. Further concern was provided by the broken arm sustained by goalkeeper Steve Conroy in the Anglo-Scottish Cup semi-final replay at St Mirren on 3 December. Reserve Neil Ramsbottom, an experienced 'keeper, who had been signed in October, was drafted in for the next two games but proved inadequate to the task. As a result, manager Harry Haslam paid £50,000 for Derek Richardson from Queen's Park Rangers, and he made his debut in United's 2–0 victory over Southend on 21 December.

With the goalkeeping position looking less than secure, the Blades were also experiencing a worrying lack of goals. Jeff Bourne and Barry Butlin had proved to be an effective front pairing in United's early good run: the team had scored 24 goals, with the two strikers contributing 11. Yet the Blades had only scored 12 goals in their next eight games, only four coming from Bourne and Butler. It was clear, therefore, that the balance of the team was not quite right. This seems to have been illustrated by the fact that United's promising run in the Anglo-Scottish Cup had been ended by a crushing 4–0 defeat at St Mirren, and Grimsby had then convincingly beaten United 2–0 in the second round of the FA Cup at Blundell Park on 15 December. Blades boss Harry Haslam believed that the season could still be put back on track, however. United's early great run still meant that they were on top of the table and, starting with their Boxing Day fixture against neighbours Wednesday at Hillsborough, the Blades would face three promotion contenders in succession, as afterwards Grimsby and then Blackburn would visit Bramall Lane.

The game at Hillsborough was to prove a disaster. Mick Speight was injured in the first half and substituted, the Blades were a goal down at half-time and then routed by Wednesday in the second half. A 4–0 scoreline was a huge blow to morale and by no means an ideal preparation for the visit of Grimsby three days later. Missing Mick Speight, with damaged ribs, the Blades would also have to replace John Cutbush, substitute for Speight at Hillsborough, who had sustained a badly-bruised foot. Haslam decided to bring Tony Moore into the problematic right-back slot, and although Moore had only made a handful of appearances, the manager was confident that he would perform well. Fortunately for the stability of the Blades defence, John MacPhail would be able to continue at centre-half, passing a late fitness test prior to the game.

Haslam was aware that Grimsby would offer a stiff test for his players. The Mariners had already knocked the Blades out of the FA Cup and a home victory over Barnsley on Boxing Day had moved them up to second place, just one point behind United. Grimsby had been promoted from Division Four the previous season and had made a solid start to life in the Third Division. Their potential was clearly displayed by an excellent run in the League Cup, where they had beaten Scunthorpe, Huddersfield, Notts County and First Division Everton to reach the quarter-final, where they had taken another First Division side, Wolves, to a replay before finally being knocked out. Under the shrewd management of George Kerr, Grimsby were developing into a good footballing unit and Kerr confidently asserted, prior to the game, that 'We've got up to second place on merit and we don't fear anyone.' Nevertheless, the Mariners would be without key players Kevin Kilmore and Kevin Drinkell upfront and Johnstone in defence. Publicly, at any rate, Haslam was also appearing confident: 'I still think we're on the right road, despite the Boxing Day match. One result doesn't make us a bad side.' In reality though, it was not just one result; United's form had not been good since the end of October. Now, crucially, the Blades had to silence the critics and restore pride and confidence in both themselves and the fans. It was a crunch match, a pivotal game, and a good performance and result was essential.

Sheffield United: Richardson, T. Moore, Tibbett, Kenworthy, MacPhail, Matthews, de Goey, Bourne, Butlin, Garner, Sabella. Substitute: Brown

Grimsby Town: Batch, D. Moore, K. Moore, Waters, Wigginton, Crombie, Brolly, Ford, Liddell, Mitchell, Cumming.
Referee: Mr M. Glover
Attendance: 21,684

The early exchanges were fast and furious, befitting a game of such importance, yet it was to be the visitors who settled down to play the more measured and constructive football and so begin to dominate the game. Mariners skipper Joe Waters, Bob Mitchell and Mike Brolly were particularly prominent in this period, and only sterling defensive work by the Blades kept the pressure off 'keeper Derek Richardson. There was a degree of forcefulness about Grimsby, however, and there were heavy tackles on Alex Sabella and Paul Garner as the quarter-hour mark approached. Awarded a free-kick for the foul on Garner, John Matthews hit a fierce right-foot shot from the edge of the Grimsby area, which 'keeper Nigel Batch dived at full length to push around the right-hand post.

Failing to apply any pressure from the resultant corner, the Blades were soon in trouble themselves as full-back Tony Moore was caught in possession by Grimsby's Gary Liddell, but then recovered to knock the ball out for a corner. Brolly took the kick, Richardson came and punched out, but only to Bobby Mitchell, who knocked it back into the area. With United hesitant in moving out, Clive Wigginton was on side as he headed the ball back across goal for the unmarked Bob Cumming to head the ball past Richardson for the opening goal, with 17 minutes on the clock. Spurred on by their success, the visitors began to play with even greater confidence. But the Blades, despite finding it hard to create any sense of rhythm in this period, did not give up, and Len de Goey sent Moore away down the right and, from his cross, Butlin headed the ball down for Jeff Bourne to fire over the bar. Shortly after, Barry Butlin almost had the equaliser, only smart work by Batch keeping out a fierce volley from the United striker.

Gradually, as the half approached its last 10 minutes, United, prompted by the industrious, hard-running and strong-tackling Paul Garner, began to impose themselves on the midfield. With 36 minutes gone, the Blades won another free-kick just outside the Grimsby area. Sabella touched the ball off to de Goey, who hit a fierce shot, which Batch was equal to and punched away. Almost immediately, Grimsby broke rapidly. A free-flowing move ended with Richardson bravely diving to take the ball at the feet of Tony Ford, the Grimsby player cautioned by the referee for following through on the United 'keeper. Into the last five minutes it was the Blades who were certainly getting the upper hand, with Bourne and Garner forcing Batch into further good saves, the Grimsby 'keeper playing an increasingly influential role in the game.

As the second half got under way, United quickly showed their determination to get on level terms. Garner, battling for the ball in midfield, won it and then sent Bourne away with an incisive pass. Riding a couple of tackles, Bourne sent a great ball into the box, Butlin diving in to head just wide of the post. With Grimsby's ability to counter-attack quickly on the break, the Blades had to be on constant alert, and only a brilliantly-timed tackle by Len de Goey stopped Cumming from putting the visitors 2–0 up. Yet most of the pressure was coming from the Blades and after 53 minutes they were level. Paul Garner, breaking into the Grimsby area, was taken down by Wigginton and a penalty was awarded by referee Glover. Jeff Bourne, who had missed his last spot-kick against Southend, showed no signs of nerves as he smashed the ball past Batch to make it 1–1. A minute later Bourne flashed a shot across goal then, at the other end, from Brolly's corner, Waters headed just wide of Richardson's net.

At this point, Alex Sabella, who had been subdued in the first half, really began to show his class, and one run in particular had the Grimsby defence at sixes and sevens as he weaved through the challenge of a number of defenders and into the opposition area. But to United's misfortune, there was no one there to add the final touch as Alex played the ball across goal. With the Blades now well on top, Garner almost found Bourne with a great cross from the left, only for Wigginton to head it clear. With 20 minutes to go, Jeff Bourne, injured in a clash with Wigginton and Crombie that required stitches in his leg, was taken off by Haslam and replaced with young striker Dougie Brown. The youngster was to prove troublesome to the Mariners defence as he sent in two good shots just wide of the goal. Yet even though Sabella continued to torment them, the visitors were determined to hold out and were unwilling to buckle under increasing Blades pressure.

With three minutes to go, United almost had it won, as substitute Dougie Brown hit a fierce volley that had Batch grasping at thin air, only for the ball to fly an agonising few inches wide of the post. A minute later the game climaxed in a moment of real controversy as John MacPhail went to ground with Grimsby's Gary Liddell, the latter kicking the United man as he got to his feet. There followed a mêlée of players and a yellow card for MacPhail, while Liddell was sent off. It was a sour note on which to end a pulsating game, and controversy followed as an altercation began among the players in the tunnel after the game.

A draw had been a fair result and both managers were pleased with their team's performance. Grimsby boss George Kerr was happy with his team's domination of the first half, but he acknowledged that the Blades had proved stronger over the 90 minutes and that Alex Sabella was indeed 'a great player'. For Haslam, the game justified his claim that the Hillsborough match had not suddenly made his side a bad one. Yet *The Star's* Pritchett, like many United fans, wondered, 'why on earth didn't United play like this when it really mattered, at Hillsborough?'

It was now felt that the Blades should use this performance to find the consistency of performance they had displayed earlier in the season. As Peter Hegarty of the *Telegraph* noted, 'United's encouraging display kept them at the top of the table. If they can consistently reproduce their second-half form, promotion should be assured.'

United's next game saw further optimism. Blackburn were beaten 2–1 on New Year's Day in front of another crowd of over 20,000 at Bramall Lane. Yet that effectively was that. Top of the division on New Year's Day, the Blades won just three of their next 20 League games and finished in a disappointing 12th position. Barry Butlin missed the month following the Blackburn game, Jeff Bourne departed to Atlanta four months later and there was a real inability to score goals. Injuries at key times to Len de Goey, Les Tibbott and John Matthews certainly did not help the team in terms of continuity and experience. With the goalkeeper position also uncertain, it was always going to be difficult for United to continue their promotion push. Yet form was still very poor; 10 out of the last 20 games were lost and Unitedites were well aware that without their good start to the season the team could certainly have been relegated.

United's team of the 70s

Given that the decade divides into two distinct periods, one of success in the campaigns up to 1975 and of decline thereafter, clearly any 'best 11' is likely to be heavily weighted towards those players who performed well in the early part of the decade. As such, the choice of players was made easier. Two positions did prove more competitive across the years, however: a striker to play alongside Billy Dearden and someone to play on the left side of midfield. In addition, while still a First Division side United had two Scottish goalkeepers of real class – Tom McAlister and Jim Brown. A difficult choice between them, ultimately I chose McAlister, given his brilliance at such a young age. Had 'Tommo' not suffered the broken leg that ultimately wrecked his United career, he would have had every opportunity to become a goalkeeping legend like Alan Hodgkinson.

Up front, there were players who had made an impact during the early period, such as John Tudor and Jim Bone, but their stay at the club during the period was not long enough to warrant inclusion. Keith Edwards did create a club scoring record during the 1976–77 season, but he was less effective the following year and was then sold by Harry Haslam. Given that Keith's great United days came in the following decade, when he had fully matured as a striker, my choice fell on Gil Reece. Although Gil is perhaps remembered more as a winger than a striker, he always had an eye for goal and, when given a 'free role' up front by John Harris in the 1970–71 season, was a key component in United's final promotion jigsaw. Ultimately, Gil Reece in the early 70s was a more potent striker and played at a higher level when compared to the younger Keith Edwards of the later 70s.

On the left side of midfield, Gil Reece was unavailable, given his inclusion as a partner for Billy Dearden and, although Geoff Salmons was an excellent player in the top flight, his goalscoring record was poor, while Stewart Scullion, who could be brilliant on his day, was inconsistent. From the later 70s, the choice thus fell between Gary Hamson and Alex Sabella. The former made great progress from an early age and proved his quality by moving on to top-flight Leeds after United's relegation in 1979. Ultimately, however, Hamson did not have the exceptional skills of Sabella, whose misfortune as a United player was to play in teams where few of his colleagues shared his level of ability and speed of thought. Alex would surely have thrived in United's early 70s team.

Below are biographical details about the chosen 11. Hopefully, the match reports that specifically relate to each of these players will give more of a flavour of their presence and abilities on the football pitch. As ever, football is a game of opinions, and readers who watched the Blades in the 70s will probably disagree with some of the choices. If that raises debate about the relative merits of different players, then all well and good. As long as we continue such debates, the players of this great decade can never be forgotten.

Manager: John Harris

For Blades fans who have watched United since the 1960s, John Harris commands total respect and there can be no question that he stands head and shoulders above United's other managers in the 1970s and, many would argue, is undoubtedly the club's greatest post-war manager.

John was born in Glasgow in 1917. His father Neil was a Scottish international centre-forward. A promising young player, John was signed by his father, manager at Swansea, in 1935. He moved on to Tottenham and then Wolves in 1939. Initially an inside-right or wing-half, John switched to centre-half, guesting there in two wartime Cup Finals for Chelsea. Signed by the Blues for £8,000 in 1945, the same year saw him represent Scotland against England. He was made captain at Chelsea and then won the League title in 1954–55 with the Blues – the highlight of his playing career. In 1956 John became player-manager of Chester, moving on to Bramall Lane in March 1956 to replace Joe Mercer.

John's great managerial achievement was in seeing United through the huge transformation in the game created by the abolition of the maximum wage in 1961. This magnified the division in the game between the bigger, wealthy clubs and those like United, whose resources were more limited. With a three-sided ground and only one seating stand, United's directors knew that ground development was essential to generate the revenue to keep the Blades at the top level. Consequently, little money was available for transfers and Harris knew that he would have to focus on home-grown players and bargain buys. Consequently, a succession of excellent youngsters like Mick Jones, Len Badger, Alan Birchenall, Alan Woodward and Geoff Salmons complemented cheap, but brilliant signings such as Keith Kettleborough, Gil Reece, Billy Dearden and Tony Currie. Additionally, in the promotion seasons of 1960–61 and 1970–71 when the team faltered, the astute Harris made key signings – Len Allchurch in 1961 and Trevor Hockey in 1971 – to ensure that the team went up. Most importantly, Harris produced teams of real attacking flair, with the Blades spending nine out of 13 seasons in Division One, achieving a position of fifth in the top flight in 1961–62, which has not been bettered since.

Harris was a product of the 'old school'. No media man, he shunned personal publicity, talking only about his team. His honesty and integrity were legendary, gaining him the title 'Gentleman John'. In the swinging 60s, however, expectations were high; not everyone appreciated Harris's decency or the handicaps he faced. Managers were now expected to deliver success, regardless of circumstances. The true reality of United's situation was apparent at the start of the 1967–68 season, however, when Harris had to accept the sale of key strikers Jones and Birchenall – for £100,000 each – and the season culminated in relegation.

After a year as general manager, Harris returned to lead the team at the start of the 1969–70 season. Disappointingly, promotion was not won, but Harris dealt brilliantly with the pressure of expectations in the ultimately successful campaign of 1970–71. The respect of older Blades for Harris is in no small part due to his attacking philosophy and his desire to find creative talents who could blend together to produce hard-working, tough and exciting displays. Yet tactically, Harris was very astute. He recognised that in some games play had to be kept tight and he ignored the hecklers who targeted Frank Barlow, bringing the defensive midfielder in for several tricky away games. Harris would frequently utilise his players – Hemsley, Reece, Tudor and Barlow, for example – in different positions to confuse the opposition. The fact that United were so well-respected and played with such flair in winning promotion is in no small way due to 'Gentleman John'.

Describing the Blades boss, the West Ham's match programme of 6 November 1971 declared, 'John is the only bachelor among First Division managers. He leads a simple life – brown bread, honey and black coffee is his favourite breakfast – but in an interview stated, "I'm married to the club, that is my life. There is no time for anything else."'

Feeling that United needed a younger, more modern-minded manager, John stepped aside for Ken Furphy in December 1973, later going on to scout for neighbours Sheffield Wednesday.

Goalkeeper: Tom McAlister

The merits of Scottish goalkeepers has been much debated south of the border, yet in the early 70s United believed that, in one young Scot, they had found the classy performer who would finally assume the mantle left by legendary Blades and England 'keeper Alan Hodgkinson.

That young man was Tom McAlister. Born on 10 December 1952 in Clydebank, 'Tommo' first came to the attention of the scouting fraternity, it was said, playing between a couple of coats in a kickabout in a local park. Joining the Blades in November 1969, the Scot quickly impressed the Lane's coaching staff and a year later enjoyed a successful run in the reserves following an injury to second-choice 'keeper Graeme Crawford. At the end of United's promotion season of 1970–71, Crawford had moved to Mansfield and Tom was now deputy to John Hope, who had recently taken over from the legendary Alan Hodgkinson.

At first Hope had done well, playing the final 17 games of the season and proving a reliable 'keeper as United took the First Division by storm in the opening stages of the 1971–72 season. Yet, as the season progressed, his form and confidence suffered, culminating in a disastrous home performance against Arsenal on 29 January when the Blades lost 5–0. Concerned, manager John Harris took advantage of a break caused by United's early exit from the FA Cup to try out McAlister in a couple of friendlies against an Israeli XI and Dynamo Kiev. Explaining the decision, the club stated, 'Mr Harris said that he felt playing Tom in Tel Aviv and against Kiev would give him a couple of chances of gaining experience in top-class football. It had not gone unnoticed that Tom had kept a clean sheet in six of his last seven Central League games.' With a return to League action Harris bided his time and recalled Hope. Tom, however, was finally brought in for his League debut at Ipswich in a goalless draw on 15 April 1972. Impressing, he kept the goalkeeping jersey for the final three games.

Tom started the following season as first choice, having just failed to gain a winner's medal in the popular pre-season tournament, the Watney Cup. Tom had been unable to save a penalty in the 7–6 shoot-out defeat to Bristol Rovers, which was ironic as he later gained a reputation as a penalty-saving expert when he stopped two of Derby County 'hot shot' Alan Hinton's penalties at the Baseball Ground in October. The 1972–73 season saw him ever-present in United's net and a firm favourite with the fans. Just 21 years of age and seen as Scotland's next 'keeper, his future seemed assured. Unfortunately, when Tom went down to save at the feet of Manchester City's Rodney Marsh at the Lane on 20 October 1973, he broke his leg. Immediately, Harris signed Manchester United reserve John Connaughton as cover. Connaughton would not have been a long-term challenge, but, in March 1974, new boss Ken Furphy signed Jim Brown – another class Scottish 'keeper – from Chesterfield. His brilliant performances, and the fact that McAlister's recuperation was prolonged, effectively meant that after recovery Tom moved on to Rotherham United in January 1976, having played his final game against Middlesbrough on 26 December 1975.

Tom made 159 appearances for the Millers in Division Three, then moved on to represent Blackpool, Swindon and Bristol Rovers. Signed in May 1981 as cover for West Ham's England goalkeeper Phil Parkes, Tom went on to make 85 appearances for the Hammers, turning in some excellent performances at the top level which recalled the excellence of his youth.

Right-back: Len Badger

Len Badger was born on 8 June 1945 and was one of the last players to join the club as a member of the 'ground staff' – the apprenticeship scheme was introduced the following year. This required him to sweep and clean all areas of the stadium and even saw him being sent to the top of the old floodlight pylons. A local lad from Attercliffe, he graduated from the Coleridge Road school team to represent Sheffield, Yorkshire and England schoolboys. Self-effacing, Len recalled that luck had played a key role in his progress. At Coleridge Road

he had played as a right-half or inside-right. For Sheffield Boys, these positions were filled and he was moved to right-back, so marking out his future career.

In reality, Len progressed because he had real ability, a factor that Blades boss John Harris quickly noted. Len made his first competitive start against Bury in the League Cup in October 1962 and his First Division debut in the 2–0 home victory against Orient on 26 April 1963. This followed his success with England – along with fellow Blade, Bernard Shaw – in winning the European Youth

Championship. So impressive was the youngster, that he was quickly brought into the England Under-23 squad. Len represented the Under-23s on many occasions, captaining the side, as well as representing the Football League.

By the end of March 1964 Len had replaced stalwart Cec Coldwell as United's right-back. Made captain of the side in succession to Joe Shaw in early 1966, he was the youngest skipper in the top flight for some time. A full-back of real quality, Len was skilful, fiercely competitive and had great powers of recovery. He was particularly noted for his attacking qualities, which greatly complemented the exciting style of play of the United team of the Currie–Woodward era.

There were disappointments for Len. He never gained a full England cap – a fact that amazed most within the game, but not Sheffielders, who felt that the city's players were always too readily overlooked. In addition, he never won a major trophy with the Blades and was devastated when the team was relegated in 1968. As he later recalled, 'I had a good start to my career, then suddenly it ran away. Gone was the glamour of playing at Highbury and Old Trafford. There's only one place to play – and that's the First Division.' His greatest moment, therefore, was promotion in 1971 and a return to the top flight.

Coming from a fanatical Blades family background, it is not surprising that Len stayed loyal to the Blades, while others, at the height of their powers, moved on. Undoubtedly United's best post-war full-back, the *Green 'Un's* Peter Howard described Len, during his testimonial season, as 'a son of Sheffield, who has been, and still is, a credit to United and the city.'

Left-back: Ted Hemsley

United's full-back pairing of Len Badger and Ted Hemsley came together on 1 November 1969 in the home game against Blackburn. Bar injuries, the pair were a fixture in United's

team until March 1975, and they were an essential part of United's success in the promotion season of 1970–71.

Ted Hemsley had a different route into United's first team than local boy Badger. Born on 1 September 1943, Ted impressed at both football and cricket while at school and was to end up having a first-class career in both games. Playing county cricket for Worcestershire, Ted became the last in a long line of cricketing footballers to play for the Blades. Ted joined Shrewsbury Town and made his League debut on 29 April 1961 at Bradford City when he was 17. Ted was a midfielder under Arthur Rowley at Shrewsbury, and was Rowley's first signing when he took over as manager at the Lane in August 1968. With Rowley's departure at the start of the following season, Harris returned as boss and, shortly after, switched Ted to left-back. Like Len Badger, Ted was quick, eager to support the attack, able to deliver quality crosses from the flanks, as well as being excellent in the tackle and in his covering and marking. As a pair, Badger and Hemsley were outstanding: clearly the best in the division during the promotion season. Ted was voted the Supporters' Club Player of the Year in 1973 and was a valued player under the management of both John Harris and Ken Furphy. Following the arrival of Jimmy Sirrel as manager in October 1975, Ted quickly found himself out of favour and made just five further appearances for the Blades in over a season and a half. In July 1977 Ted moved on to Doncaster Rovers.

Centre-half: John Flynn

John Flynn made his debut for his home-town club, Workington Town, at the age of 17. He was Arthur Rowley's last signing as United manager, costing a fee of £5,000 in July 1969. On his arrival at the club, John Harris had again taken over as manager, and in Flynn's first season he found himself making 16 (1) League and Cup appearances as a deputy for first-choice centre-half David Powell. During the 1970–71 season, Flynn found himself unable to break into the first team, given the solid central-defensive partnership of Eddie Colquhoun and David Powell. A serious knee injury sustained by Powell at Queen's Park Rangers – which effectively ended the Welshman's United career – provided a real opportunity for John to establish himself in the first team. This he did, playing in the final seven games of the promotion campaign and, in the process, establishing himself firmly as Colquhoun's defensive partner; the two men were the strong heart of the United defence for several seasons.

Flynn was a key member of the team that stormed to the top of the First Division at the start of the 1971–72 season and stayed at United until May 1978. Strong, fast and good in the tackle, John was superb in the air, a real presence in both penalty areas. Dangerous at corners and set pieces, John scored eight goals in 185 (5) League appearances.

Centre-half: Eddie Colquhoun

Scotsman Eddie Colquhoun began his professional football career at Bury, making his League debut in October 1963. In early 1967 Eddie was signed by Jimmy Hagan, manager of West Bromwich Albion. Sustaining a broken leg, Eddie missed out on the Throstles FA Cup Final victory in 1968 and, after recovering from injury, found it hard to regain his place in the side. Arthur Rowley persuaded Eddie to drop down from the First Division and join United for £27,500 in October 1968, a fee that made him a real bargain. Made club captain a week after his arrival, Eddie became the rock at the heart of the Blades defence. Quick, strong in the tackle and commanding in the air, Eddie was a real danger in the opposition penalty area from free-kicks and corners, and scored 21 goals in 360 (3) League appearances.

During the 1970–71 promotion season, Colquhoun provided outstanding leadership through some very difficult games and periods, and he continued his brilliant run of form that extended back into the previous season. Importantly, Eddie, following a period of on-the-field disciplinary problems, was now, at 25, a more mature and seasoned professional. Back in the First Division, Eddie proved his real quality and was to miss just a handful of games over the five seasons that United remained in the top flight. Eddie was to leave the Lane in March 1978 for Detroit Express in the North American Soccer League.

Right-midfield/winger: Alan Woodward

Born on 7 September 1946, Alan Woodward was discovered playing for Barnsley Boys by United's chief scout, Archie Clark. Signed as an apprentice in April 1962, he won the Northern Intermediate League and Cup with United in 1964. Under the guidance of

Eddie Edwards, who looked after the Juniors, and coach John Short, 'Woody' made rapid progress, making his first-team debut at 17 in the County Cup against Rotherham in April 1964 and later scoring in the 4–3 defeat of Barnsley in the Final. It was not long before the young winger made his First Division League debut against Liverpool at Anfield on 10 October 1964. He scored his first League goal in his fifth appearance at Leeds. The player adapted quickly to the demands of top-flight football and had reached 50 appearances – scoring 10 goals – by the end of the 1965–66 season. The following season saw him well-established in the team, as he played 41 out of 42 games, scoring an impressive 11 goals.

Blessed with immense natural ability, 'Woody' spent much time working on his technique after training. He was a direct winger who put over brilliant crosses for a succession of forwards – Mick Jones, Colin Addison, John Tudor, Gil Reece, Billy Dearden – but was also keen to cut inside, or run on to a defence-splitting pass to blast a blistering shot past a string of nervy opposition 'keepers. Blades fans were convinced that he had the hardest shot in football. His set-piece skills were especially impressive. He was a good deliverer of free-kicks and corners, scoring directly from the latter – most notably, as recorded on *Match of the Day*, at Leicester in September 1971.

The 1967–68 season saw United relegated, but was fortunate for Woodward as it also saw the signing of young Tony Currie from Watford. It was the burgeoning partnership between the two that was the main feature of United's early 70s team. The players combined to create scoring chances for themselves and others, and they developed clever routines at set pieces – especially the ploy of a Currie long corner, played to the edge of the area, for Woodward to rush in to meet with a crashing volley. For a winger, Woodward's goalscoring feats were exceptional. He was top scorer for seven seasons, hitting a total of 158 League goals – second only in Blades history to the legendary Harry Johnson.

Following United's relegation from the First Division, Woody was made United's captain and led the side for the following two seasons. Unfortunately, at the start of the 1978–79 season, issues away from the pitch led Alan to seek a move to the United States, where he played for Tulsa Renegades. Alan's last competitive match for United was in the 2–0 defeat at Fulham on 9 September 1978. His loss was keenly felt by United, and had he remained in the side it is difficult to see United suffering the humiliation of relegation to the Third Division at the end of that traumatic season.

Unfortunately, although 'Woody' had many admirers in the English game and represented the Football League in 1971–72, he never received a full England cap – further convincing Sheffielders that the city's clubs were being ignored by the national side. He was idolised by the fans, however, and is the only Blade to win the Player of the Year award on four occasions: 1970, 1974, 1976 and 1978. Alan Woodward is a true Blades legend.

Central-midfield: Keith Eddy

Keith Eddy joined his home-town club Barrow, making his Football League debut at the age of 16 in September 1962. In July 1966 he was signed by Watford's player-manager Ken Furphy, who would later link up again with Eddy at Bramall Lane. At Watford, Keith captained the side to the Third Division Championship and a FA Cup semi-final. Prior to the start of the 1972–73 season, John Harris signed Keith from Watford for £50,000. Keith's first kick for United was a successful penalty, taken as a substitute in the shoot-out that decided the Watney Cup Final against Bristol Rovers at Eastville.

Almost 28 years of age, Keith had never played in the First Division before, and fortune was not to favour him in his first few months at the club. Starting the first three League games of the season, Keith had tendon trouble and his leg was put in plaster. Back in the side for a League Cup replay against Charlton in early October, he was forced straight back into plaster and did not reappear in the side until the 3–0 victory over West Bromwich Albion – a relegation 'four pointer' – on 6 January. Having seen little of Keith, some supporters wondered if, with his lower League background, he would be up to the task. They need not have worried, as John Harris had utilized his talent-spotting skills again. Eddy, his injury cleared up, was to hold his place for the remainder of the season and increasingly became a key, influential member of the side and a major reason United were able to pull clear of relegation trouble and finish the season in mid-table respectability.

Keith was a confident player; despite the early setbacks, he had no doubt that he would succeed in the top flight. Importantly, Keith was assured and commanding in midfield and assumed a leadership role within the team. He was a great complement to the skills of Tony Currie, was able to play the holding role and was strong in the tackle and combative in the air. In addition, he had the ability to use the ball well, showed creativity and was able to get from box to box, as shown by his Goal of the Month in front of BBC's *Match of the Day* cameras at White Hart Lane on 18 January 1975. Furthermore, Keith was also a superb central-defender; Ken Furphy remarking that he wished he had two Keith Eddy's – one to play in midfield, one to play at the back!

After Furphy took over from John Harris in December 1973, the new manager appointed Keith the team's penalty taker instead of Alan Woodward. A surprising decision to most Blades fans – given Woodward's great rate of success – but Keith did the job well.

During the successful 1974–75 season, Furphy took the team captaincy off Tony Currie, to enable him to shed the additional responsibilities and focus on his creative role within the team, and handed it to Keith, who proved an excellent choice.

With the disastrous start to the relegation season of 1975–76 and the sacking of Ken Furphy in October, it was not long before Keith departed to join his old manager – and Pele – at New York Cosmos, having played his last competitive game for the Blades at Coventry City on 10 January 1976.

Central-midfield: Tony Currie

On 4 September 1973 United hosted Arsenal in the First Division. Four goals up after 17 minutes, the Blades ended up 5–0 winners, reversing the Gunners victory by the same scoreline at the Lane in January 1972. The game is remembered for the actions of Blades midfield maestro Tony Currie, who, having scored two goals, sat on the ball near the end as revenge for Alan Ball's similar humiliation to the Blades in that earlier fixture. Of United's players that night, only 'TC' would have had the confidence and arrogance to make such a statement. He was a player at the height of his majestic powers and his actions further strengthened the affection Blades fans felt towards him.

Currie, just turned 18, was signed by John Harris from Third Division Watford for £26,500 in January 1968. An England Youth international, he had attracted the interest of several clubs. With United fighting a First Division relegation battle, the youngster was seen as one for the future. He soon entered first-team action, however, scoring on his debut against Tottenham in a 3–2 victory on 26 February. Currie went on to play 13 games and, although the team were relegated, he was now well-established in the side.

By the promotion season of 1970–71, Currie's class was clear for all to see and he had added physical strength and consistency to his undoubted skill. His performance and stunning goal against Don Revie's Leeds United in the League Cup in September 1970 was a portent of what the top flight could expect. In United's breathtaking start to the 1971–72 season, Currie was outstanding and, although the team faded, Currie's 40-yard blockbuster past Liverpool's England 'keeper, Ray Clemence, remains a highlight of the season. TC's form was recognised by Alf Ramsay, who gave him his England debut against Northern Ireland at the end of the season. The selection pleased fans on both sides of the Sheffield, who felt that players at both Sheffield clubs had been too long neglected by England.

Following interest from Manchester United during the 1973–74 season, Currie signed a five-year contract at Bramall Lane. The intention was to create a succesful team around the England star, but building the South Stand left the club with few resources to carry out the plan. The Blades enjoyed a swansong season in 1974–75, however, finishing sixth: one point off UEFA Cup qualification. The season saw Tony's brilliant solo goal against West

TONY
CURRIE

Ham eulogised by BBC's John Motson as 'a quality goal by a quality player'. Unfortunately, the disastrous 1975–76 season saw 'TC' become increasingly frustrated and the subject of transfer speculation. With relegation, Currie moved on to Leeds for £245,000.

The abiding image of 'TC' is of a great entertainer – blowing kisses to the fans, while dribbling the ball towards the opposition. Yet he was a serious team player who, while leaving a legacy of genius, never neglected the game's basics. Chelsea's Ron Harris said, 'he is the ideal midfield player; his strengths are his confidence, control and non-stop work rate.' In particular, Currie combined well with Woodward and Dearden up front and was the perfect midfield complement to the terrier-like Trevor Hockey. Most of all, 'TC' was the Blades' last truly 'great' player: the last player about whom different generations could argue the relative merits of – in Currie's case the inevitable comparison being with Jimmy Hagan.

Left-midfield: Alejandro (Alex) Sabella

Second Division Sheffield United were the focus of the back pages of the national newspapers in July 1978, thanks to the activities of manager 'Happy Harry' Haslam out in Argentina. At a time when English football had not begun its romance with foreign players, Haslam had shown daring and initiative in being the one English manager to see the potential of signing players from the country that had just hosted and won the World Cup. Initially, Haslam had been interested in World Cup winners Ossie Ardiles and Ricky Villa. When Tottenham became alerted to their availability, however, Haslam, unable to match the £700,000 now needed to secure them, arranged their transfer on the Londoners' behalf. Haslam was not finished, however, and on 19 July announced the record signing of Alejandro 'Alex' Sabella for £160,000 from South American champions the River Plate Club. The 23-year-old attacking midfielder was an Argentine international, who Haslam hoped would develop into a better player than Ardiles or Villa.

Haslam placed great expectations on Sabella; he would be the key playmaker around which the team would revolve, yet, importantly, he stressed that 'he isn't here to carry the club'. Unfortunately, the reality proved different. Alex soon demonstrated that he had superb skill, control and the ability to make penetrating runs, and with Haslam's introduction of coaches Danny Bergara and Oscar Arce, there was clearly an intention to build a team capable of producing South American-style football. Yet, sadly, too few of United's players had the ability required. Alan Woodward departed for the USA, Keith Edwards had been sold, and promising youngsters Imre Varadi and Simon Stainrod were to be sold before the season's end. Haslam had signed Chelsea striker Steve Finnieston, but the player was injury-prone. Perhaps only Peter Anderson, with 12 goals in 28 games, linked effectively with Sabella.

At the start of the 1978–79 season, Alex and the Second Division Blades defeated European champions Liverpool in the League Cup but also lost three of their first five League games. Haslam noted that, although 'Alex is doing his stuff, we really want someone looking to finish off what he is starting.' Yet it did not happen and, ultimately, the season was a disaster, with United dropping into the Third Division. Following relegation, Second Division Sunderland reportedly offered £600,000 for Alex, but Sabella, wanting top-flight football, stayed. United topped the Third Division at Christmas 1979, but fell away to a mid-table finish. At the season's end, Leeds manager Jimmy Adamson bought Alex for £400,000. Adamson was soon sacked, however, and Sabella, not favoured by new boss Allan Clarke, eventually returned to Estudiantes in Argentina in January 1982.

Alex clearly found English football physically tough, yet he still played 76 out of a possible 88 League games and there was no shortage of clubs wanting to sign him. The artful Sabella was also a marked man in the days before the game's laws offered a measure of protection to such gifted individuals. Blades fans were shocked by relegation in 1978–79 and so, perhaps, Sabella's reputation as a star player suffered because of it. It is worth remembering, therefore, that Tony Currie was unable to save United from the drop in 1975–76, nor was Jimmy Hagan in 1948–49.

Striker/centre-forward: Billy Dearden

As a youngster, I remember being delighted to open *Shoot* magazine to see a photo spread entitled 'Billy Hits the Hammers 1-2-3'. The caption referred to a Billy Dearden hat-trick in the 3–0 Lane victory against West Ham in February 1971. The victory gained some revenge for the 5–0 thrashing inflicted upon the Blades at Upton Park in the League Cup back in November.

Born in Oldham on 11 February 1944, Billy joined his home-town club, but did not turn professional until completing his plumbing apprenticeship at the age of 20. In December 1966 he moved to Crewe and then to Fourth Division Chester. Joining United for £10,000 in April 1970, most Blades fans assumed that, at 26, he had been signed to strengthen the squad, not as a first-team regular.

Manager John Harris, though, was a shrewd judge of potential. As an outside-right, Dearden had scored 22 goals in 85 League games for Chester. Moreover, others were tracking him and, but for luck, he could have ended up elsewhere. Manchester City's chief scout Harry Godwin had watched Billy, recalling that 'here was a good player who could do well in the First Division.' City's coach Malcolm Allison went to Chester to watch Dearden, ready to open transfer negotiations. However, a knee injury meant that Billy did not play, and when Allison decided to wait, the Blades pounced. Their offer, according to Godwin, 'surprised a lot of people, but not us.'

So how was Dearden transformed from a lower division journeyman into one of the country's top strikers? Harris recognised that Billy had great pace, could find and exploit space and finish effectively. He thus switched him to centre-forward, where he thrived on the quality service provided by Currie in midfield and Woodward, Reece and Salmons on the flanks.

In his first season, United gained promotion and Billy played a key role by scoring 14 goals in 40 (1) League appearances. His equaliser in the final away game at Middlesbrough

was crucial, as were his two strikes in the following victory against promotion rivals Cardiff. Initially, Dearden operated as a joint striker with John Tudor. Tudor joined Newcastle in January, however, leaving Billy as United's sole recognised striker. Adequately supported by goals from others – especially Woodward, Currie and Reece – Dearden operated confidently in the role. *The Star's* 'Promotion Souvenir' congratulated the 'Oldham lad with tremendous guts, considerable skill, sense of humour and admirable temperament.' The reference to 'tremendous guts' was especially apt. Bill suffered from serious cartilage problems, often only training on two days a week and regularly having his cartilage pushed back into place at half-time, before he could have an operation at the end of the season.

Following promotion to the top flight, Dearden kept on improving. In 1971–72 he scored 16 in 35 League games, and in 1972–73 scored 20 in 37, the last Blade to achieve the 20-goal benchmark in the top flight. Briefly, he also struck up a productive partnership with Scottish striker Jim Bone, signed from Norwich for £30,000 in February 1973, the pair adding 11 goals in a nine-game period and pulling United clear of relegation trouble.

Yet, unfortunately, the injuries persisted – he had three cartilage operations all told – and in 1973–74 he played just 20 times. The 1974–75 season saw an improvement in fitness, as Billy played 31 (3) times, scoring 8 goals. Yet it was clear that injuries had deprived him of his previous speed and sharpness. When United were relegated in 1976, Billy managed just 7 (1) appearances, scoring in his final game against Manchester United in December 1975.

At 5ft 10in and weighing under 11st, Dearden, like Keith Edwards and Harry Johnson, proved that a top striker does not have to be a big man. In 170 (5) League games, Billy scored 61 times, mostly in the top flight, an excellent strike rate. To supporters who remember the early 70s team, Billy Dearden will always remain one of United's greats.

Striker/winger: Gil Reece

Gil Reece was born in Cardiff on 2 July 1942, but failing to make the grade at his home-town club, signed for Newport County, where he made his League debut in October 1963. After playing 32 games for Newport, Gil was signed by John Harris for £10,000 in April 1965. Gil made his first-team debut shortly after, on 3 May, scoring two goals in a 4–0 win at Doncaster, which landed United the County Cup. Reece had been bought as a left-winger and quickly established himself in the side at the start of the following season, 1965–66, adapting well to the challenges of the top flight and fitting in well with a number of other talented young players who would emerge over the next couple of seasons, such as Len Badger, Alan Birchenall, Mick Jones, Ken Mallender, David Munks, Bernard Shaw and Alan Woodward.

Although small – just 5ft 7in – and slight – around 9st 9lb – Gil was an extremely tough competitor. A fierce tackler, he was quick, skilful, could deliver good crosses and, for a small man, was tremendous in the air, scoring many of his goals with headers. In fact, Gil's goalscoring record, 59 goals in 197 (14) League appearances, is an excellent strike record for a player signed primarily as a winger.

Gil broke his leg in November 1966 and missed most of the rest of the 1966–67 season. Returning for the 1967–68 campaign, Gil was back as first choice and personally had a good season, being the club's top scorer with 13 League goals, yet the team suffered as United were relegated to the Second Division. The 1969–70 season again saw Gil as the club's top scorer with 14 League goals and a crucial Cup goal in United's magnificent victory over Everton in the third round of the FA Cup at Bramall Lane on 3 January 1970.

The promotion season of 1970–71 saw Gil start the campaign but then lose his place to Geoff Salmons at the start of October and start just one League game in the next 17, either finding himself on the bench or left out of the matchday 12 all together. Selected for the away League game against Oxford United on 30 January, Reece was given a new 'free role' in attack. It was another brilliant decision by manager John Harris. Gil and United's attack was rejuvenated, as the Welshman went on to show some of his best-ever form for United and played a major role in the securing of promotion with some key goals and brilliant

performances. The highlight for Gil was probably his two-goal performance against Birmingham City at Bramall Lane in the 3–0 victory on 17 April. Gil turned in a star performance and was applauded from the field by his teammates. In United's post-season promotion souvenir 'Together to the First', Reece's contribution to United's success was summed up thus: 'His brilliance was a major factor in promotion being clinched. It is doubtful if the Welsh international has ever displayed better form than that shown in the promotion run-in.'

Yet, during that same season, Gil, a man renowned for speaking his mind and not suffering fools gladly, had seemingly brought his international career to an end. Chosen in November as part of the Welsh squad to face Romania, Gil walked out when left out of the team, declaring, 'I'm fed up with being messed about. I'm not going to be a glorified bootboy.' Given his continued good form, Gil was to be forgiven by the selectors. He eventually won a total of 29 Welsh caps, 18 of them with United.

Injury kept Gil out of the starting line up at the start of United's 1971–72 season and new signing Stewart Scullion took his place out on the left. A great start by United to the season made it initially difficult for Gil to get back into the side, but his ability as a striker was amply demonstrated as he effectively covered for the injured Billy Dearden during October and November, and then returned to the left for a run of games following Billy's return. Yet Gil was finding it harder to keep his place in the side and, although involved at the start of the 1972–73 season, he played his last game for United in the 3–1 victory over Southampton at the Lane on 2 September. Shortly after, a transfer deal saw Gil and David Powell return to Wales in an exchange deal for Cardiff City striker, Alan Warboys.

Bbliography

This book has been written with the aid of the following sources:

Newspapers

The Sheffield Star

The Morning Telegraph

The Green 'Un

The Western Mail

The South Wales Echo

The Daily Express

The Daily Mirror

Club Programmes and Publications

Sheffield United's official programme through all its different guises 1970–79

Together to the First: Sheffield United's official promotion souvenir for the 1970–71 season

Arsenal Official Programme, 24 August 1971

Blues News. Birmingham City Official Programme, 12 August 1972

Cardiff City Official Programme, 3 December 1977

Everton Official Programme, 19 April 1975

Forest Review, 4 September 1971

Leicester City Official Programme, 18 September 1971

Manchester United Review, 2 October 1971 and 23 April 1973

Norwich City Official Programme, 3 April 1976

Tottenham Hotspur Official Programme, 18 January 1975

Books

Armstrong, Gary and Garrett, John *Sheffield United FC. The Biography*

Clarebrough, Denis *Sheffield United Football Club. The First 100 Years*

Clarebrough, Denis and Kirkham, Andrew *A Complete Record of Sheffield United Football Club 1889–1999*

Farnsworth, Keith *Sheffield Football. A History. Volume 2 1961–1995*